Family Therapy

with Older Adults & their Families

Family Therapy

with Older Adults & their Families

Alison Marriott

WINSLOW

Winslow Press Ltd
Telford Road, Bicester, Oxon OX6 0TS

Dedication

This book is dedicated to my father Vincent Murray, who died aged 60 years, during its writing. I would also like to acknowledge the love, support and influence of my mother, Dorothy, and my children Holly and Erin.

About the Author

Alison Marriott works as a Consultant Clinical Psychologist for Central Manchester Healthcare Trust and is Head of Clinical Psychology Mental Health Services for Older Adults in Manchester. In addition to her clinical work she has published in the areas of Family Therapy, Depression, Resettlement and Elder Abuse.

First published in 2000

Winslow Press Ltd, Telford Road, Bicester, Oxon OX6 0TS, UK

www.winslow-press.co.uk

002-2624/Printed in the United Kingdom/1010

British Library Cataloguing in Publication Data

Marriott, Alison
    Family therapy with older adults & their families. – (Winslow editions)
    1. Family psychotherapy
    I. Title
    616.8'915
ISBN 0 86388 232 3

Contents

Acknowledgements

I AM COMPLETELY INDEBTED to my friends and colleagues of the Central Manchester Family Team, who have helped to develop my ideas and challenge my thinking either as present or past members of the team since its inception in 1984; particularly Susan Benbow, Stuart Walsh, Mark Johnson, Jean Hyde, Ken Garrod, Mike Morley, Adam Pickles, Jude Wells, Ann Quinn, David Egan and Kath Tregay and to all the families I have had the privilege to work with.

My thanks, too, to Graham Stokes and to Stephanie Martin for their comments upon the draft, and to the Prudence Skynner Family Therapy Team for Older Adults, Pathfinder NHS Trust, London, for their permission to use the last exercise in the book.

CHAPTER 1

Introduction

THIS CHAPTER INTRODUCES THE ISSUE of working with older people and their families. It considers areas such as, *who* is the family and *where* and *how* may we work with families? It goes on to consider a number of situations where family work may be particularly appropriate within services for elderly people. Many of the issues raised in this chapter are further developed later in the book.

Our relationships with other people are among life's most important experiences. We love, we embrace, we mourn and we hate. As a result of this, we sometimes feel elated and we sometimes feel lonely. Life is a continuous process of growth, transition and deterioration. (Perlman, 1988)

We have significant relationships with many people within our life span. Relationships with friends, intimate partners, work colleagues and bosses, schoolteachers and, of course, members of our family all make important contributions to our development. Family and systems therapy involves working with families and systems of relationships between individuals as the main focus for change and development, rather than taking an individual perspective, which focuses upon the development of the person as an individual per se. Family therapy traditionally addressed the early phases in the development of the family, when issues surrounding the parenting of children and adolescents are centre stage. Older family members attended family therapy services less often and were rarely the focus of intervention. Interest in the later stages of family development has emerged more recently, and various services, including the one with which I work in Central Manchester, have flourishing family therapy services for older adults and their families. These services emphasise the importance of the family and other relationships in later life in both precipitating difficulties for family members and in allowing change and growth to occur.

Family Relationships in Later Life

When contemplating a family approach, an assumption is sometimes made that many older people have limited contact with family members, but in fact the converse is usually true. Although a shift towards smaller family size tends to mean that older people have fewer children than they used to have, national surveys in the United States have found that only 3 per cent of elderly people have no relatives at all, and there is some evidence that older people have *more* contact with their families as they age. One study of elderly people living in a rural setting in Wales found that about half of the older people with children, and a third without children saw a relative *every day*. Children were the family members most often in contact with parents, but contact with brothers and sisters tended to increase in later life, especially after the age of 75 years and after widowhood (Wenger, 1984). At this stage of the life cycle, when parents are likely to be dead, brothers and sisters may be the only remaining generation with whom older people can reflect and reminisce about past shared life experiences in the family, and this may play an important function. Contact with siblings often increases when they coordinate resources to care for an ageing parent, and this may well set a pattern of increased sibling contact, which continues after the death of the parent.

Contact between grandparents and grandchildren often plays an important role in the lives of many older people. Between two-thirds and three-quarters of people aged over 65 years have grandchildren, although grandparenting can be a very diverse experience reflecting the wide range of years in which someone can become a grandparent: potentially from their early thirties to their early nineties. It may also be a diverse experience in families where separation, divorce and remarriage have altered the ways in which older family members have contact with children and grandchildren. Increased longevity has also had an effect upon late-life family experiences and has increased the likelihood that family members will encounter the late life-cycle events of great-grandparenthood and perhaps even great-great-grandparenthood.

Many factors play a role in determining the closeness or otherwise of family relationships. The nature of the kinship relationship is important, and various factors such as geographical distance and occupational commitments may influence the frequency of contacts. The quality of the relationship in earlier life is also likely to be important to the nature of the relationship in later life. Gender plays an important part in family relationships, and this relates to the different roles which men and women may have in families, and how the roles may change as family members age. Some aspects of family relationships are influenced by the ageing process more directly, and one example of this concerns marital roles. As a result of the greater longevity of women, only 22 per cent of women over 75 years have a surviving partner, in comparison with 68 per cent of men. This statistic, in itself, has implications for who is most likely to need and to provide family care and support for older men and women in families. However there are also gender differences in the provision of family care for older parents, and daughters are much more likely to fulfil the role of primary carer than are sons.

Family contacts and relationships are therefore very important and significant to many older men and women and family therapy approaches recognise this by working with the older person and their family system rather than with the older person alone.

Who is the Family?

Since our family clinic for older people and their families began to operate in Manchester in 1984, we have had the opportunity to meet a wide range of families facing a wide range of challenges. There have been a number of areas in which it has been particularly helpful to work with the older adult *and* their family, and some of these areas will be addressed later in this chapter. However, before considering how working with families may be useful, it is important to be clear about *who* the family is and *who decides* which family members will be invited to attend a family meeting.

Within our service we tend to identify the family in different ways. We generally begin by asking the older adult who they would like to invite to the family appointment. However, this can be difficult if the client has memory or other cognitive difficulties, or if they seek to exclude or protect a family member by not putting forward their name, when from other perspectives the person may seem to have an important contribution to make. These issues may need to be resolved by discussion with the elderly person and/or other family members.

We then write to each identified family member, inviting them to attend, irrespective of their geographical distance from the older person, and also invite each person to bring along anyone else who they feel may have an important contribution to make. A standard letter describing the service is also sent. Sometimes this practice means that people who are not family members attend, but they are nevertheless people who at least one member of the family has felt to be important to the family system. They may be neighbours, friends or other professional carers. Sometimes family members will contribute in their own way, other than by physically attending a family meeting. They may, for example, telephone to make a verbal contribution, or may send a letter. The way in which family members contribute to the family meeting may often help us to understand some aspects of communication style and interaction within the family, and sometimes family members may choose to provide information to a family meeting in ways which are less typical. Within our family clinic relatives have sometimes chosen to attend for only part of a meeting or have even communicated a contribution to a family meeting by fax. Sometimes family members will travel long distances to attend, reinforcing the view that, whilst geographical distance may reduce the frequency of contact with an older family member, it does not necessarily lead to emotional distance.

Apart from identifying *who* to invite to a family meeting, there are other important issues to consider too, such as *where* to see the family, *when* to meet, and *how* to work with the family.

Where to Meet

When considering *where* to meet the family, there may be a range of options, but the choice is usually between the home of a family member and a service base. Many services for older people are flexible in terms of where a service is delivered and often see clients in a range of settings for individual work. When conducting a family meeting, there are a number of potential advantages in seeing families in the home setting: the family may feel more relaxed in their home setting, and it may increase the chances of convening more of the family, as the setting may be more accessible, particularly for frailer elderly people. A meeting in the home environment may yield more information about the social and environmental circumstances of the family, and it may also help to identify the home setting as a place in which discussion of important issues can occur. It may therefore focus change in the family's own home setting. On the other hand, if the home of the older adult is the meeting place, it may not necessarily be a place in which other family members feel comfortable about meeting. It may represent a place in which adults 'grew up' as children in the family, rather than a place where adults can develop in the family as adults. If the home is identified as a place of conflict, where a particular balance of power exists between family members, this may also affect a family meeting which occurs in the home, and it may be preferable to invite the family to the more 'neutral' territory of the service base.

There are some potential benefits to seeing the family at a service base: it may be more convenient for clinicians, particularly if the service is in a rural area where large travelling distances between family appointments are involved; it may be argued that the family have more choice about attendance if the appointment is at an office base, and that it may be an imposition upon some members of the family to arrive at their home if they do not wish to join other family members at the appointment. In order to attend an appointment at a service base, the family will also have to organise themselves and be sufficiently motivated to attend. On the other hand, this can be a disadvantage when working with families with a family member who, because of mental health difficulties or cognitive impairment, may not have insight into the potential advantages of attending for an appointment, but where the advantages to the person and the family of attendance may be considerable. Sometimes the family may perceive an appointment at a service base as more 'special' and it may therefore have more impact upon the family.

In many respects the decision about where to meet will probably reflect an agreement reached by the family and staff according to the particular circumstances and situation of each family. Within our service in Manchester we have encountered families with clear preferences for either home or service-based appointments and have tried to meet in accordance with this.

When to Meet

In much the same way, when deciding when to meet, the service will usually benefit from adopting a flexible approach. Whereas work with individual clients involves negotiating an appointment with only one person, negotiating a family meeting involves taking account of the needs and contingencies of other family members too. However, many family members will often make considerable efforts to attend a family meeting if they feel it will be helpful.

Services offering family appointments operate in many different ways, but generally our service in Central Manchester tends to have three main ways of working with families, which also sets a pattern for the frequency and location of meetings with families.

Family Assessment Meetings

This method involves inviting a family to an assessment meeting, where they discuss with a group of clinicians or 'family team' discuss ideas and thoughts about a particular situation which the older adult and their family are encountering. This may lead to further family meetings or may often be a 'one-off' session which leads to a plan of action which can be fulfilled without further family appointments; and it may lead to contact with other parts of the service or other agencies instead. It is often an opportunity for the family to get together with staff to think about difficult issues and can be time effective in terms of decision making about care planning. Sometimes an assessment meeting may be used to reassess a client with their family from a different perspective. In such a case, a member of a multidisciplinary team may feel they have become 'stuck' with a particular situation and may ask for a family assessment meeting, which draws upon the expertise of colleagues, to help to generate new ideas about how the situation may be helped. The clinician may then continue to work with the client(s), using some of the new ideas, and this use of a family meeting involving other colleagues may therefore help to support individual clinicians in continuing to work effectively with particular clients.

Therapeutic Family Meetings
This often involves meeting the family for a period of 'assessment' and discussion of the main issues, but is then followed by a period of continuing to work therapeutically with the family. Within our service this may be for only a few sessions or may be for a more lengthy intervention period. The number of sessions for therapeutic intervention with elderly people and their families in our service has ranged from two to nineteen meetings. Meetings usually occur approximately once a month, but there is considerable variation. Sometimes meetings may be much less frequent than this, although the client may be in contact with other parts of the service (day hospital, CPN service and so on) between appointments.

Family Crisis Intervention
A number of families who attend for family meetings may attend for several sessions, often fairly close together, following a particular event or crisis which affects the family system. Contact may then end, but in some cases the family or a referring agency will contact the service again at some future point, if further difficulties arise, and a similar brief intervention is offered. This latter pattern is one which our service has often encountered with families facing longer term and more enduringly difficult situations, where difficulties tend to re-emerge and continuing adjustment is necessary. Examples of this would be families where an older adult has a chronic physical illness or dementing illness; and families where there are long-standing difficulties in domestic situations, such as where continuing alcohol problems or domestic violence impinge on the life of the older adult in

the family, as these situations tend to increase the likelihood of family crisis points occurring.

How to Work with Families

There are many different ways of working with families and forms of family intervention, which are to some extent determined by the theoretical approach of the clinician, the nature of the presenting difficulty and other resources. Texts by authors such as Barker (1983), Burnham (1986), Griffin (1993) and Street & Dryden (1988) describe some of these approaches and some of the main schools of family therapy. The various schools of family therapy adopt differing theoretical positions, as is the case with individual psychotherapies, and adopt different ways of working with families.

Many family therapy services draw upon different theoretical approaches when working with families. Some services working with late-life families work as a multidisciplinary family team, whereas other clinicians work mainly alone, consulting colleagues when appropriate. In the service with which I work a number of families are seen in their own homes, sometimes by a lone member of staff. This may begin as a fortuitous meeting with family members who are at the home of the elderly person when an individual assessment appointment has been arranged in the home following referral. Typically this would involve contributions by the family members to the assessment process and, in gathering information about the elderly person, it would allow a more comprehensive assessment to occur. However, with some families, it may be appropriate to move on to offer therapeutic family appointments in the home of the elderly person, where other family members are invited to attend, and where the therapist may draw upon colleagues to participate in the family meeting too.

However, we also have a more formal family therapy service which operates for one session every week. This family clinic is organised by a multidisciplinary team of staff, and the older person and their family are invited to our service base. Staff contributing to the family clinic have been drawn from a wide range of professions over the years and, at present, staff whose professional training is in clinical psychology, psychiatry, nursing and social work are among team members. The structure of sessions is more formal than for work outside the specific clinic, and is influenced to some extent by the work of the Milan team, and also by the ideas of Tom Anderson (1990) concerning reflecting teams, which are described more fully later in this book (see Chapter 6). This more formal family clinic setting is often used with families where issues have arisen which appear to be more complex or difficult.

The following sections describe the way in which the family clinic operates and the roles of members of the team, and may be seen as one way in which clinicians working with families may structure a family service.

Roles of Family Team Members

Two members of the team, co-therapists, meet with the family in one room and the remaining team members are a support team, who sit in a separate room, connected by a video and telephone link. One of the members of the support team has the role of peer consultant. The peer consultant's responsibilities are the following:

- to coordinate the session
- to write letters to referring and other agencies
- to pass messages using the telephone link from the support team to the therapists during the family meeting.

Interventions made using the telephone link may be to suggest that the therapists ask a particular question or explore a particular issue with the family. Sometimes several interventions of this kind may be made during a family meeting, but at other times there may be none. All roles in the team rotate, so that different team members may take the role of therapist, peer consultant and support team each week. However, if families are seen more than once, the same therapists would meet them on each occasion.

A video recording of the session is made, if the family consent to this by signing a video consent form. This is kept as a record of the session for future evaluation, and sometimes for teaching other professionals, if the family have agreed to this use. Although some families are initially concerned about different aspects of this process, for example the thought of observers in another room, or the use of video, very few families remain concerned when the process is fully explained to them, and an explanation of the method of working is sent to all families prior to their attendance at the clinic.

The structure of a typical family meeting in the family clinic is outlined below, with approximate timings, as an example of one formal way of working with families.

Outline Family Clinic Meeting

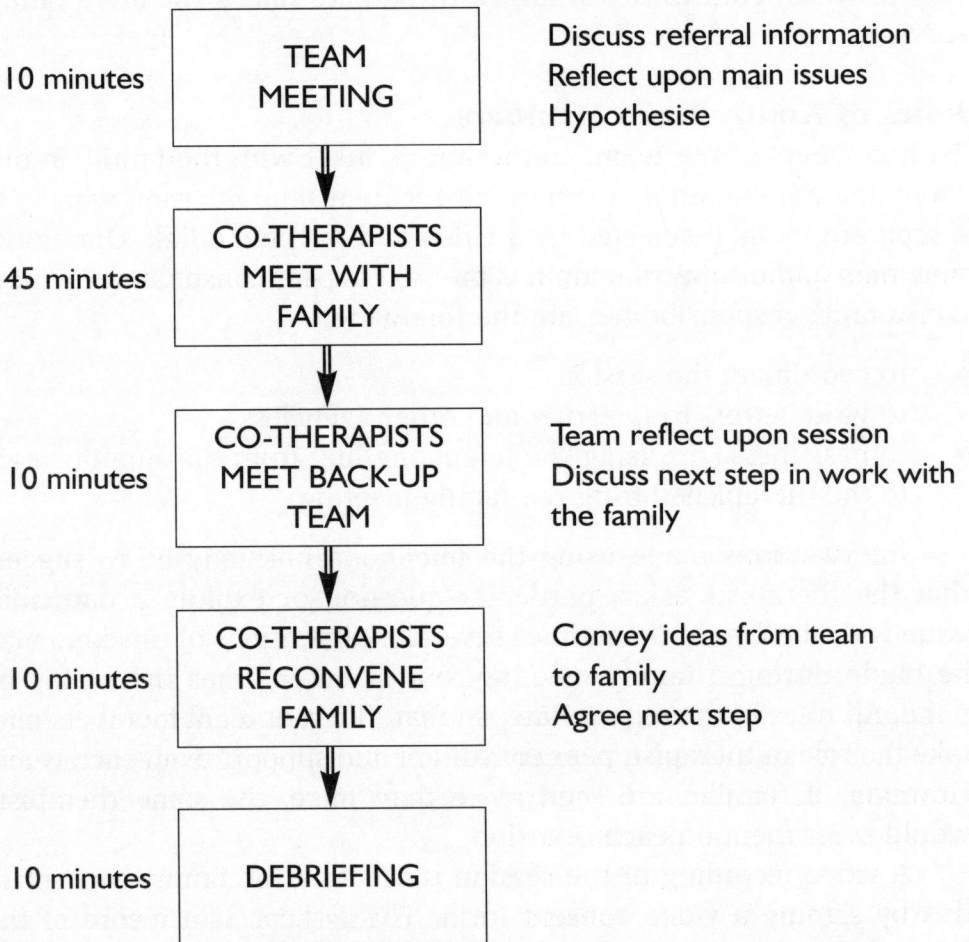

10 minutes	**TEAM MEETING**	Discuss referral information Reflect upon main issues Hypothesise
45 minutes	**CO-THERAPISTS MEET WITH FAMILY**	
10 minutes	**CO-THERAPISTS MEET BACK-UP TEAM**	Team reflect upon session Discuss next step in work with the family
10 minutes	**CO-THERAPISTS RECONVENE FAMILY**	Convey ideas from team to family Agree next step
10 minutes	**DEBRIEFING**	

This outline of one form of family meeting shows how the team meets to discuss initial referral information about the family, to reflect upon the main issues and to form initial hypotheses. The co-therapists then meet with the family to explore some of the issues and hypotheses. This is followed by a break or pause when the co-therapists leave the room to reflect upon the session with the team, and to consider how to proceed with the family. The co-therapists then reconvene the family, meeting with them briefly to reflect back the perceptions and ideas of the team, and to agree the next step. The family then leave and the team have a debriefing session, where the co-therapists and peer consultant reflect with the team about how they felt the session went, and how they felt within their role with the family.

When a clinician receives a referral concerning an elderly person, a decision may need to be made about the form of assessment which is to be undertaken, and whether this will involve a meeting with the individual elderly person, or with the person and their family. Within our service we have found that there are a number of circumstances in which it may be particularly appropriate to work with elderly people and their families, rather than with the elderly person on their own, and some examples of this are described below.

Transitional Life Events

Family therapy approaches have often been used when families are facing transitional life events. These can be events which disrupt the family system and require some adjustment on the part of members of the family in order for a new balance to be established. Some life events are likely to have effects upon particular members of the family at particular ages and stages of the life cycle, such as the birth of a child, a child starting school, a teenager leaving home, which are all events which occur at early stages of the life cycle. However other events are more likely to occur at later stages of the life cycle, and examples of this may be retirement, redundancy, bereavement and changes in physical health.

Ratna & Davis (1984), looked at the factors which were important in the referral of elderly people to an old-age psychiatry service and found that bereavement, retirement, illness or departure of a carer, and family conflict were identified as precipitating referral in 60 per cent of cases. This suggests that life events have a significant part to play in the distress of elderly people presenting to this form of service, and this could be addressed by an individual approach directed towards the elderly person themselves. However, a number of these life events may also have major effects upon the well-being of family members other than the referred person. Bereavement or loss of a member of the family or close family friend is a clear example of this, but retirement, changes in the health of a family member, and other events common in the later stages of the life cycle are also likely to affect the balance of relationships and interactions within the family. In this situation a family approach rather than an individual approach may be a more effective way of approaching the situation. A family approach may also allow the clinician to identify other life-cycle issues for family members other than the older adult, and this may be important to the family's capacity to cope with the difficulties with which the older person is presenting to the service.

In the following example illustrating four generations of a family, different life-cycle events are of particular relevance to each family member, all of which have the potential to 'feedback' and have implications for other generations of the family:

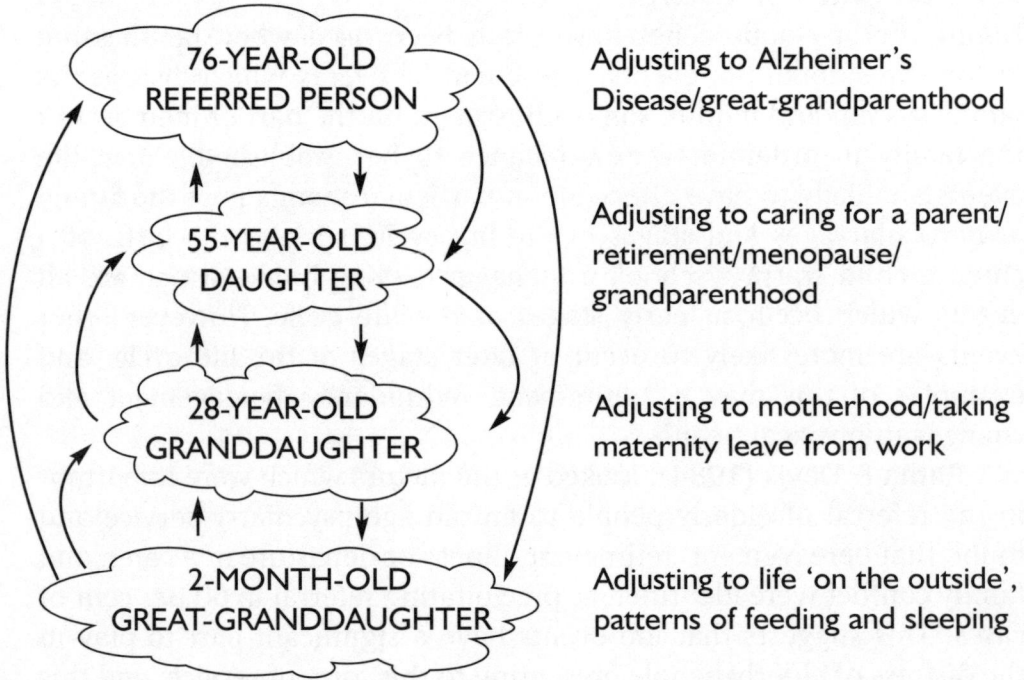

<table>
<tr><td>76-YEAR-OLD REFERRED PERSON</td><td>Adjusting to Alzheimer's Disease/great-grandparenthood</td></tr>
<tr><td>55-YEAR-OLD DAUGHTER</td><td>Adjusting to caring for a parent/ retirement/menopause/ grandparenthood</td></tr>
<tr><td>28-YEAR-OLD GRANDDAUGHTER</td><td>Adjusting to motherhood/taking maternity leave from work</td></tr>
<tr><td>2-MONTH-OLD GREAT-GRANDDAUGHTER</td><td>Adjusting to life 'on the outside', patterns of feeding and sleeping</td></tr>
</table>

Helping with Future Care Decisions

A further example of when a family, as opposed to an individual, approach may be effective concerns those situations where the elderly person is considering their future care provision. Although health, social services and other agencies have important contributions to make, the most important agency supporting the frailer elderly person is very often the family. A collaborative approach between the older person, the family and professional agencies is therefore likely to be most effective in deciding how to meet future care needs. Many elderly people who are admitted to hospital following changing health needs or difficulties at home may seek to reconsider where they will live on leaving hospital. They may be considering a move from hospital to residential care or a move from home to live with another family member. Some time ago, Duvall (1977) discussed how family work may be most appropriate at times when families are either 'contracting' or 'expanding'. This was with reference to the earlier stage of the life cycle as, for example, when a child is born the family 'expands' and when a young adult leaves home the family 'contracts'. Both of these periods were identified as times when the family system needs to adjust and when difficulties may arise. In later life, families often experience similar challenges of expansion and contraction. If an older family member moves into the home of other family members for support and care, the family 'expands' in one sense, and if an older family member dies, or moves from the family home to live in residential or hospital care, the family 'contracts'. It is therefore important that future care decisions, involving, as they often do, significant changes for family relationships and contacts, should be clearly negotiated and agreed by family members.

Sometimes elderly people may spend many weeks or even months longer than is necessary in hospital because clear links have not been established between staff and family members of the older person, which allow for clear care planning for the future to be determined. Many individuals within families find it difficult to verbalise their capacities to care for an older family member, and their feelings about the role of caring for an older family member. Assumptions can be made in these circumstances by professional staff about the capacities of family members to care for older adults which do not lead to effective support services being established in practice. Roles within the family may need to be renegotiated to incorporate an older person who has reduced skills as a result of a physical or mental health problem and professional staff may have an important role to play in working with the family to facilitate this process. Staff may also be able to help family members communicate with one another about their hopes for future care. There may often be conflict between the expectations of the elderly parent and younger family members about whether the family can provide care or how much support they can offer. Sometimes there may be conflict in roles for a family member who is proposing to provide support and care. The daughter who visits her parent regularly to offer care and support may find this causes difficulties with her partner and children, which the family find difficult to resolve. A family meeting can help to discuss and resolve opposing views in these circumstances.

Mental Health of Other Family Members

A further appropriate use of a family approach is when the mental health or welfare of a family member, other than the referred older person, is a concern. In such circumstances it may be important to address the needs of this family member, as their support and recovery may be important to the family system of which the older client is a part. A survey of families seen within our service indicated that this was a common issue for families in our clinic, and 45 per cent of families seen by our team raised concerns about the mental health of a family member, other than the identified elderly client. Concerns ranged from family members worried about stress levels or low mood in the main carer of an older family member to concerns about mental health problems such as schizophrenia in other family members. The service may be aware of some of these concerns prior to a family meeting, but sometimes the service may only become aware of these difficulties when the family attend. In some cases, although the family may have actively sought help for the older family member who has been referred to the service they may not have sought help directly for a member of the family, who can appear to the team to be even more in need. One example of this was a family where the older adult was referred by her family doctor because of low mood and the client referred obliquely to 'family worries'. When a family meeting took place it emerged that the son of the referred person was receiving treatment for a depressive illness, and the 14-year-old granddaughter, who also attended the family meeting was largely unable to participate because of what appeared to be a hypomanic illness. In this case it was necessary to arrange for the granddaughter to be seen promptly by the psychiatry service for adolescents in her own right and she was subsequently admitted as an inpatient. Her symptoms had been present for some time but the family had not consulted their family doctor about them. There are often interesting family dynamics operating in such circumstances, which usually relate to who the family feel it is most acceptable to seek help for, and who the family feel most comfortable with labelling as 'ill', particularly when mental health issues are involved.

Developmental/Life Cycle Events
There are a number of examples of the way later life families may experience difficulties when life-cycle events do not proceed as usual. Most developmental events tend to occur most commonly at particular points in the life cycle: for example, young adults leaving home in their late teens or early twenties; marriage taking place in younger adulthood. When events do not occur at the usual developmental stage, families may have difficulties because other family members are at a different stage, which no longer synchronise with one another. The example in Chapter 5 concerning Ellen and Linda illustrates this point. Linda develops her first serious personal relationship at the age of 41, at a time when her mother, Ellen, has come to expect that Linda will remain living with her for the rest of her life. Young adults 'leaving home' is an issue which often precipitates difficulties and referrals to services for younger people, but when older 'adult children' leave home it can have added consequences.

Elder Abuse and Mistreatment
A family approach may often be appropriate when actual or suspected elder abuse or mistreatment is an issue. Whereas there are clear

statutory guidelines for services to follow when child abuse is suspected or occurs, there is no legislation specifically relating to the abuse of older adults in the UK, even when the older person is perceived as being vulnerable because of cognitive impairment or other disabilities. This contrasts sharply with the situation in the United States, where all of the states have procedures for dealing with elder mistreatment. A distinction is often made between cases where (a) the care needs of the older adult are minimal, and elder mistreatment is taking place in the context of often long-standing family violence and pathological behaviour on the part of another family member; and (b) the care needs of the older adult are significant, and mistreatment occurs in the setting of a stressed family member struggling to care in the face of limited support from services.

However, in both instances, and particularly when the older adult has expressed a clear wish to remain within the family, a period of family assessment and intervention may help to develop a care plan which meets the needs of the older adult. Working with abused older adults is a stressful task for staff, and a 'family team' approach can often be an important form of support for staff working with families facing this issue. Within our own family service one of the most rapidly developing areas of referral over the past few years has been of older adults who are in family situations which are abusive or neglectful, and this probably reflects a growing awareness of this problem within services and referring agencies.

Organic Impairment and Family Needs

A final example of when family work may be appropriate is when older adults are experiencing cognitive impairment, most commonly in association with a diagnosis of Alzheimer's Disease or Multi-Infarct Dementia. The family team with which I work have reviewed our experiences of working with families where an older person has a diagnosis of dementia (Benbow *et al*, 1993), and there are a number of ways in which a family meeting may be different if it includes a family member with a dementing illness. Having the person with dementia present often helps to focus attention upon the person's needs and, in some circumstances, may allow the session to proceed more constructively, taking account of the person with dementia and their views. Sessions in which the older person with dementia is excluded may sometimes lead to other family members having more opportunity to freely describe the difficulties in caring for someone with dementia, which can be helpful in terms of stress reduction and sharing difficulties, but it may also be more difficult to maintain a focus upon the person with dementia as an individual with their own rights and needs in such circumstances. The abilities of people with dementia and the contributions they may make to family meetings may often be underestimated.

A clear case example of this was a family seen by the Central Manchester family therapy team, where the family were initially unhappy about the presence of their 84-year-old mother who had a diagnosis of Alzheimer's Disease. The family wished to meet to discuss the possibility of her main carer, the grandson, giving up his job to care for her full time. Although she was able to make little verbal contribution to the meeting initially, she was able to interject clearly, when her grandson described the difficulty he was having in reaching a decision about his job, 'I don't want that, think of yourself.' She made little further verbal contribution but her statement was very powerful. Her grandson was surprised that she still had the ability to express this view, and it helped to give him 'permission' to think about his own needs, as well as his grandmother's needs.

Amongst families seen within our family clinic, almost half have a diagnosis of a dementing illness and a number of issues are commonly raised. Whereas most of the work in this area can be done without recourse to formal family team meetings, it is sometimes helpful to utilise this sort of service if a family continues to have particular difficulties resolving issues relating to the elderly person's illness. Examples of this include challenging behaviour, when families are having significant difficulties coping with this and coordinating a way of managing it, and when negotiating who in the family is able or unable to help with caring for the older person. Other issues for families in these circumstances include how the family can incorporate a partner or parent with often vastly reduced skills into the family system, and working with feelings and fears about the illness. Many of these issues will also be relevant to families with an older adult with a physical health problem, such as following a stroke, or with illnesses such as Parkinson's Disease. Some of the fears which families have when an older adult has a dementing illness relate to concerns about the future as the illness progresses, and there are sometimes fears about whether the illness will 'run in the family', which they can usually be reassured about in a family meeting.

This chapter has introduced ideas about some ways of working with older people and their families, and some of the issues which it may be particularly relevant to address from a 'family perspective'. Just as many families may worry about being participants in 'family therapy', many clinicians worry about 'doing family therapy' and worry about whether they have the necessary skills to work with families. There are various courses which can be undertaken by clinicians wishing to develop their skills, ranging from brief introductory workshops, organised by services who have family teams for older adults, to formal qualifications in family and systems therapy. However, many clinicians working with older adults will already have considerable experience of meeting family members and talking with them in the course of their work, and may already have a number of skills which they utilise when working with families, without necessarily viewing themselves as offering 'family therapy' to family members. A range of further ideas and techniques which can be useful when working with families are introduced in the rest of this book, which may offer the reader a broader perspective on family work.

CHAPTER 2

THE FAMILY TREE:
A way of gathering information

THIS CHAPTER INTRODUCES THE IDEA of using a family tree or genogram when gathering information about the elderly person and their family. It introduces the symbols and notation used when producing a genogram and demonstrates how to use genograms to provide an 'at a glance' representation of the family. It goes on to suggest other uses of the genogram as an aid when considering relationships and themes in the family.

Tracing a family history and producing a family tree or genogram is a popular past time enjoyed by many people. In this context it is often used as a way of seeking information about family members and ancestors, their dates of birth, marriage and death, and gives a historical perspective to the family line. When working with families in a clinical setting the genogram can have similar advantages in allowing a pictorial representation of important dates and landmarks in the family, as well as having a host of other uses which help to place the needs of the elderly person in a wider context. Genograms have been used clinically by various family therapists, who often have different theoretical positions but have nevertheless found a place for the genogram in their clinical practice.

Bowen (1978) and Lieberman (1979) have often been described as major early proponents of the genogram in clinical practice, but various other people working across different schools of family theory and thought have also used them in their work, and a fairly standard style and format for recording information in the form of a genogram has been developed. Although the genogram has been used by family therapists primarily as a tool to aid the process of family assessment, there are other ways in which the family tree can be used to help the clinician to gather information.

Gathering Information using the Genogram

The genogram may be used in a number of different ways to gather information about a family, or about an individual elderly person in the setting of their family.

Summary Genograms

The clinician may receive a referral of a new client who already has extensive case notes containing large amounts of information about the client, their family and other important details of the client's history. However this information may be spread over many pages of hand-written case-notes and within numerous letters to referring agents and other services.

The use of the genogram to summarise information is likely to be particularly effective in these circumstances as it helps to gather together a large amount of information collected from the individual, and other sources. This information may have been gathered over many years but not be readily accessible because of the diverse way in which it has been recorded. The genogram may allow relevant information about the client and their family to be drawn together and detailed in a much more readily accessible pictorial form. A final draft of the genogram may be drawn upon coloured paper to help to identify this useful source of information and summary in the case notes.

It has been suggested that family doctor records could usefully contain summary genograms, particularly when several members of the same family may consult with the same practice, and a copy of the genogram could be placed in each family member's notes. The case notes of various other services may also be assisted by this use of the genogram, although the type of additional information documented on the genogram may vary according to the emphasis of the service. Old age psychiatry departments often work with clients where a wealth of family detail is gathered by various members of the multidisciplinary team, and documented across the psychiatric case notes and the case notes of other team members. Some elderly clients referred to these departments also have extensive past psychiatric case notes, from previous contacts with psychiatric services. In such circumstances the time spent producing a genogram may save future team members the task of sifting through extensive notes to clarify points of factual importance about the client and their family, but the factual information contained in the basic genogram may also be developed, as described later in this chapter, to include other important relationship, life event and thematic information relevant to the client and their family. This information may be added to the basic genogram as the client's contact with the service continues over time.

Social services departments and geriatric medicine services may also find the inclusion of a genogram useful in drawing together information about the elderly person, although the focus of the genogram may well be different in these different services. The geriatric medicine service may, for example, find that a genogram detailing family history of medical conditions across different generations is particularly useful, whereas a social services department working with older adults may find that details about main carers and the nature of relationships in the family may be more useful. This use of the genogram to describe details of the family across generations, and to portray relationships within the family, is outlined below.

This first use of the genogram to summarise information does not necessarily require that the clinician meet with the family or even the individual client specifically to draw together information to attempt a genogram. The genogram may be drawn from information contained in the case records and other records, but in such circumstances the accuracy of the information gathered and the effects of the perceptions of the recorder of the information would be particularly important issues to consider. It would always be advisable to verify details with the client and their family if, for example, a care plan was to be changed, or important changes suggested by the care team on the basis of information gathered in this way.

Genograms and the Individual

There is a further use of the genogram, which also does not necessarily require the clinician to meet the family of the client, but rather involves the clinician meeting the elderly person individually in order to produce a family tree. The clinician may use this method during the assessment process, and introduce it to the client by asking whether they feel able to help the clinician's understanding of their situation by helping to draw a family tree. The clinician could then draw the genogram in view of the client and with their assistance.

This approach is often helpful in establishing a focused dialogue between the clinician and client, and can help to develop rapport during the assessment process. The genogram provides a very visible focus which often helps the client at this stage of information gathering about the family. This may have particular advantages if the client is anxious with respect to the otherwise primarily verbal interaction of the interview process, or if the client has language or memory difficulties which are assisted by the use of a visual representation of some of the information gathering process. In addition it can help the client to feel involved and an active participant in the assessment process, which may help to establish an important precedent for the client's role in any therapeutic procedures which may follow the assessment.

Genograms and the Family

A third and more usual use of the genogram, particularly within family therapy services, is to create the genogram with several family members present during a family assessment session. This has the advantage of enabling different members of the family to contribute factual information and to express a view about relationships in the family. It can therefore help towards an understanding of interactions within the family. As when working with the individual elderly person in producing a genogram, the act of drawing the genogram often helps to establish a dialogue between the clinician and those present, and serves as a pictorial focus during the process of assessment.

In addition the clinician can often gather useful information about family dynamics and patterns of communication. When creating the genogram, the clinician may observe who says the most and the least, who expresses views strongly and less strongly, who disagrees and agrees, and who is allowed the 'final say' in the family. The clinician may gather information about whose views are discounted or ignored, and which issues produce a family consensus and which do not. Families often enjoy producing a genogram and it can therefore often be a productive means of establishing rapport and engaging them in the task of discussing a topic together with the clinician; but it must also be recognised that for some families, distressing family experiences may make the production of a genogram a difficult task for both them and the clinician. As when working with the elderly client individually, the clinician should therefore endeavour to ensure that the family are comfortable about producing a genogram, and to ensure that during the task of producing the genogram care is taken to collect information in a careful and sensitive manner.

Symbols of the Genogram

Although there are some variations in the symbols and notation used by different clinicians when creating genograms, a fairly standard form has been generally adopted to denote gender, marriage, births and death. Symbols commonly used to create the genogram are outlined below, along with specimen family trees, which gather together relevant information.

Gender

Female ◯   Male ☐

The referred 'identified' or 'index patient' (IP), is shown using a double circle or square:

Female IP ◎   Male IP ☐

Couples

It is conventional to place the male of the couple on the left and the female on the right.

Marital couple and marriage date   ☐———— M1930 ————◯

Divorce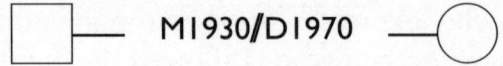

Separation

Non-married couple

Births

Children are usually placed in birth order, with the eldest child to the left, and the youngest to the right. Dates are often specified, as below, where a couple married in 1930, have a son born in 1931, a daughter born in 1934 and a son in 1940.

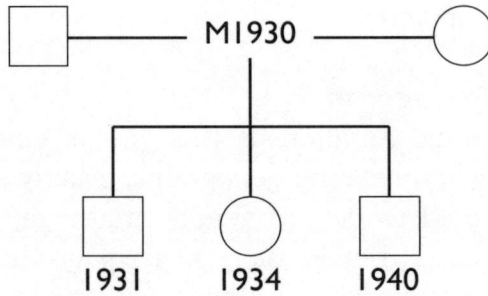

Identical twins
(monozygotic)

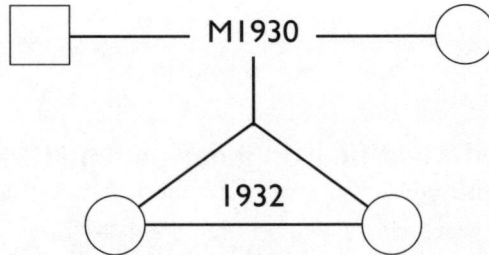

Non-identical twins
(dizygotic)

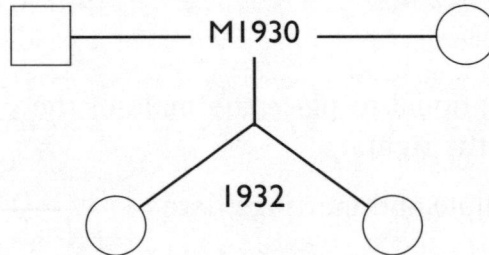

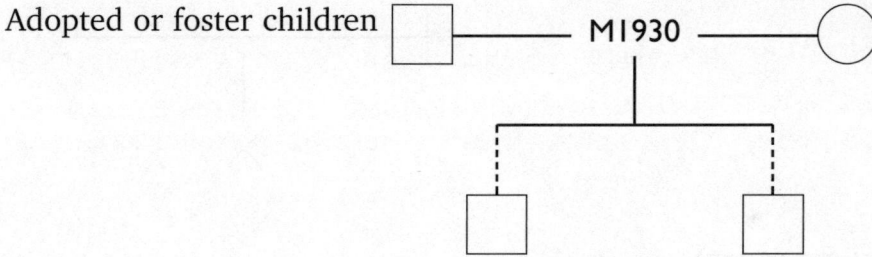

Adopted or foster children [M1930]

Death

This can be shown in various ways but the most common notation is as follows:

1910–1970   1923–1996

Additional symbols

Unspecified sex

Pregnancy

6 months

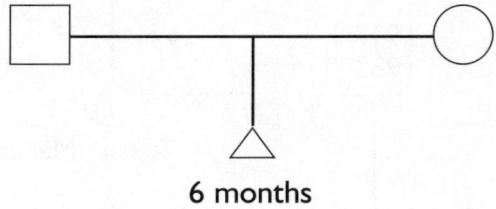

Induced termination/abortion

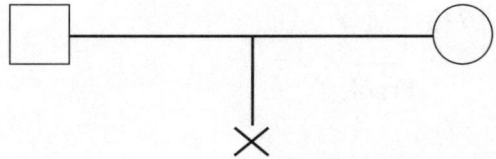

Spontaneous abortion/ miscarriage

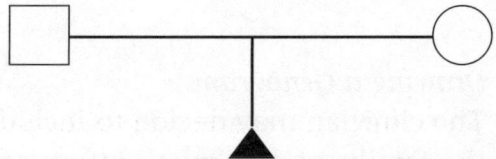

Stillbirth

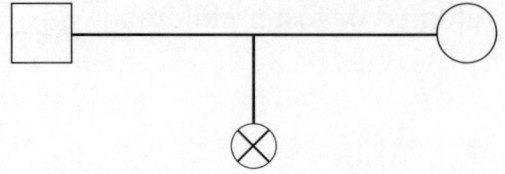

Specimen genogram

The following genogram illustrates four generations of a family and includes many of the symbols shown above:

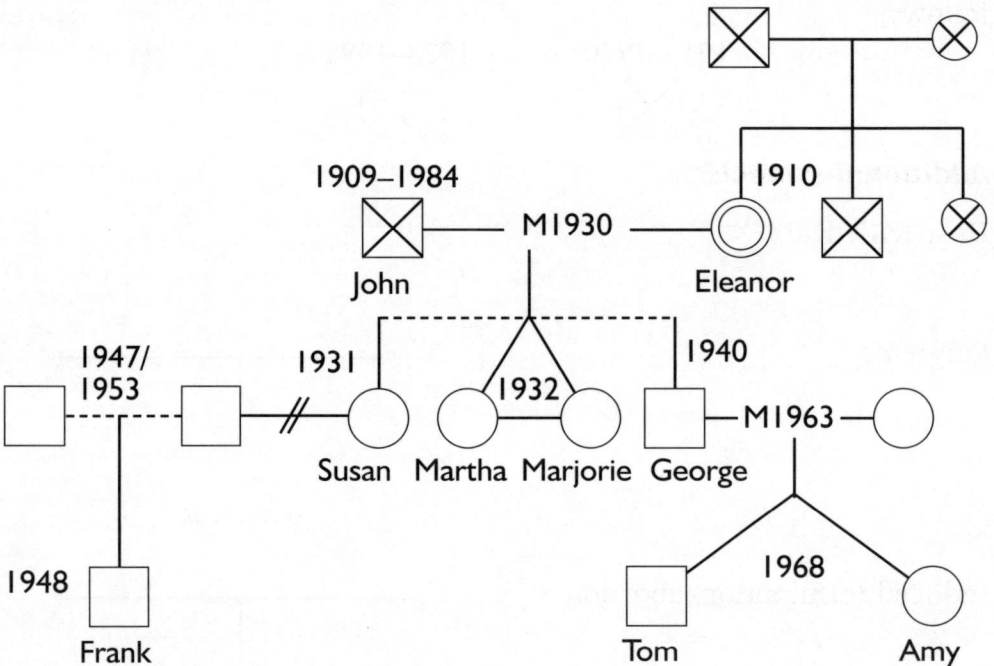

Drawing a Genogram

The clinician may decide to include as many or as few generations of the family, and as much information, as seems appropriate for each individual case. It is important that an aim of creating a factually correct genogram does not become the overriding objective if producing a genogram for a particular family was intended to serve some other function such as clarification of relationships, themes and so on, which are outlined in more detail below. The clinician may decide to concentrate only on particular individuals within the family and to collect only sparse or no details about the other members. However, in producing a factual genogram, which includes several generations of a family, it is often helpful to follow this sequence of steps:

1   Begin by drawing the referred person (IP) and their partner, where applicable.
2   Draw any children of the referred person and the partners of children. Then draw any grandchildren.
3   Move back to draw any brothers and sisters of the referred person, and the referred person's parents.
4   Repeat the last step for the referred person's partner.
5   Check that relevant names, dates of birth, marriage and deaths have been noted.

Family Relationships and the Genogram

In addition to producing a pictorial representation of factual information in the family, some clinicians find it helpful to try to represent the nature of family relationships in more detail. The following symbols are often used:

Relationships

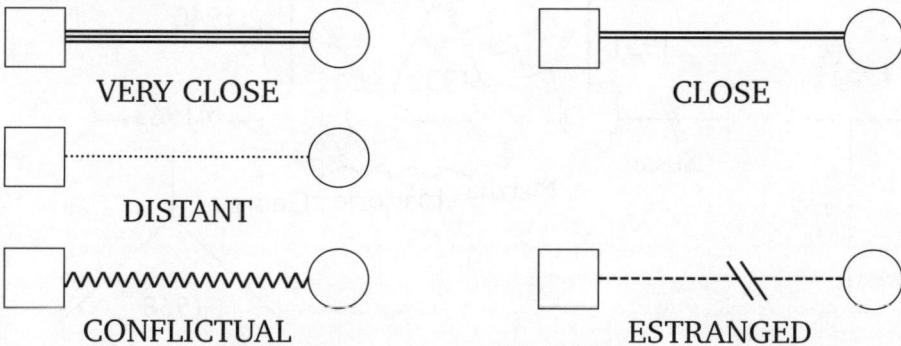

VERY CLOSE

CLOSE

DISTANT

CONFLICTUAL

ESTRANGED

Perceptions of family relationships and their nature are, of course, likely to vary considerably. Different family members are likely to perceive relationships in the family differently, and the clinician's perception may add a further perspective too. Relationships and their nature will also change over time and in relation to events and experiences. It is therefore important to recognise that a genogram which indicates family relationships is like a snapshot of the family at a particular point in time and from a particular viewpoint. Indeed engaging the family in the activity of considering relationships with the assistance of a genogram often allows a consideration of relationships and interactional patterns in the family from many different perspectives. This can be a useful exercise for the family and for the clinician too.

Relationship Patterns and the Genogram: Example
The following genogram reproduces the family tree of Eleanor and her family, as outlined above, but in this version an indication of possible relationship features has been added, using the relationship symbols.

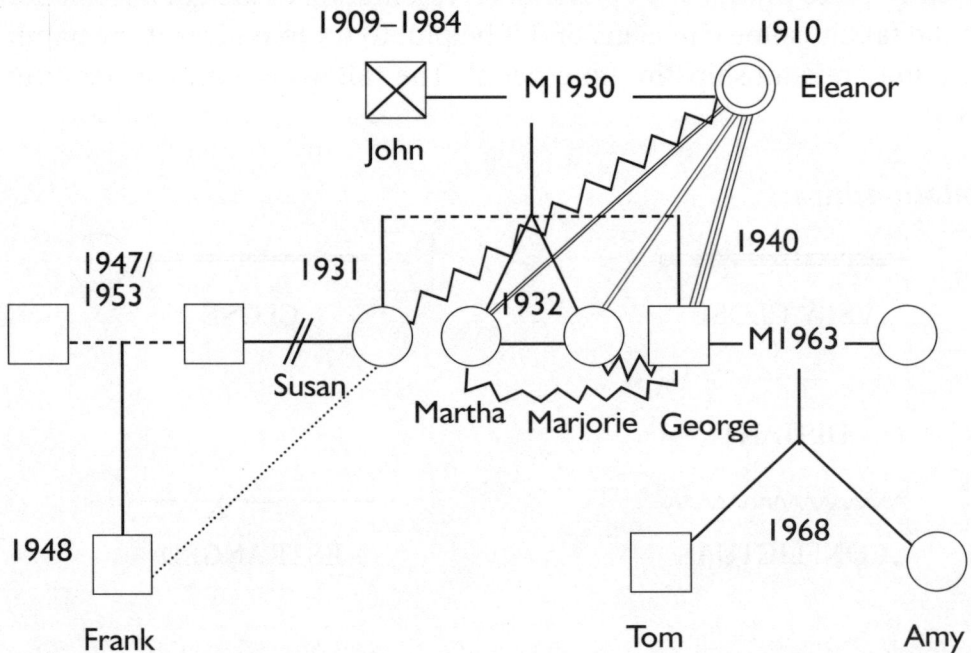

This would suggest that Eleanor, the referred elderly person, is perceived as having a very close relationship with her son, George, and a conflictual relationship with her eldest daughter, Susan. Susan in turn is perceived as having a distant relationship with her son, Frank. Marjorie and Martha are shown as having a conflictual relationship with their brother, George, but a close relationship with their mother, Eleanor.

Showing Relationships using Family Maps

A further technique for representing relationships in the family pictorially, and which can often be used in conjunction with the production of a genogram, is the use of a family map. This utilises similar forms of notation to that described above, but is also able to portray perceived hierarchies in the family. Using a family map, hierarchies are indicated by the higher or lower position of members. Relationships between family members are indicated using the notations for relationships already described above, and these are drawn between members of the family.

An example of a family map for several members of the above family may look something like this:

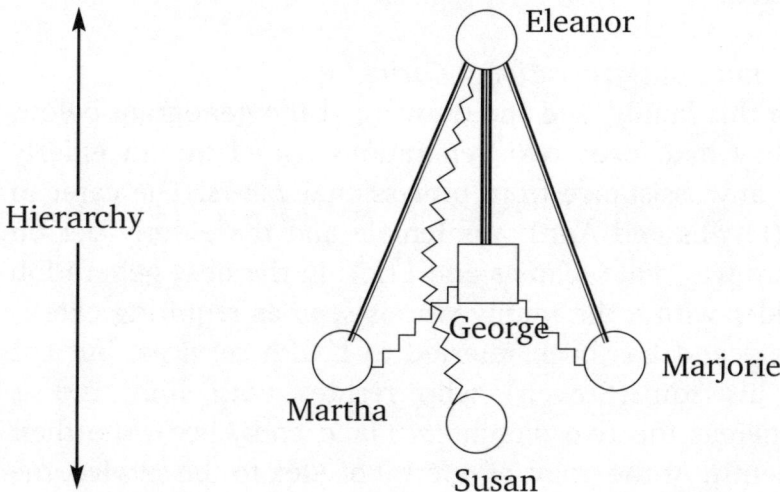

As before, the family map may be drawn in very different ways depending upon which family members are included, and whose account of relationships is used.

Family Themes and the Genogram

In addition to using the genogram to demonstrate relationships and the closeness of relationships, it can also be used to identify and to aid our understanding of important themes and beliefs within the family. There are various ways in which themes may be important in determining the family's perception of a situation and the action taken in an attempt to resolve difficulties.

Some themes may take the form of recurring patterns across generations of the family. An example of this which is often encountered when working with older people and families relates to beliefs about caring for elderly family members. A specimen genogram is presented below of a family where the issue of who provides care within the family has caused conflict and disagreement, and where creating a genogram allowed both the clinicians and the family to develop a greater understanding of how their beliefs and views about caring had developed and were influencing their situation.

This is followed by a second genogram illustrating the example of a family where perceptions about illness across have influenced the way in which members of the family feel care for their elderly mother should be delivered.

Specimen Genogram: Transgenerational Caring

Discussions with this family, and the drawing of the genogram below, revealed how they had, over two generations, cared for an elderly relative without any assistance from professional carers. The carer in both instances (Phyllis and Ann) was female and the elderly person who received care was male (James and Eric). In the next generation the identified elder within the family who is seen as requiring care is again male (Alex) and has been referred to health services, but the main carer is his son (Steven) who resides with him and is unemployed, whereas the two daughters (Jane and Alice), see their father less frequently. At the point of referral of Alex to the service, the family doctor was expressing concern because the eldest daughter, Jane, a single parent, was considering giving up her job to care for her father. However her brother Steven was very opposed to this, and felt he was coping with caring for his father, and wished instead to explore

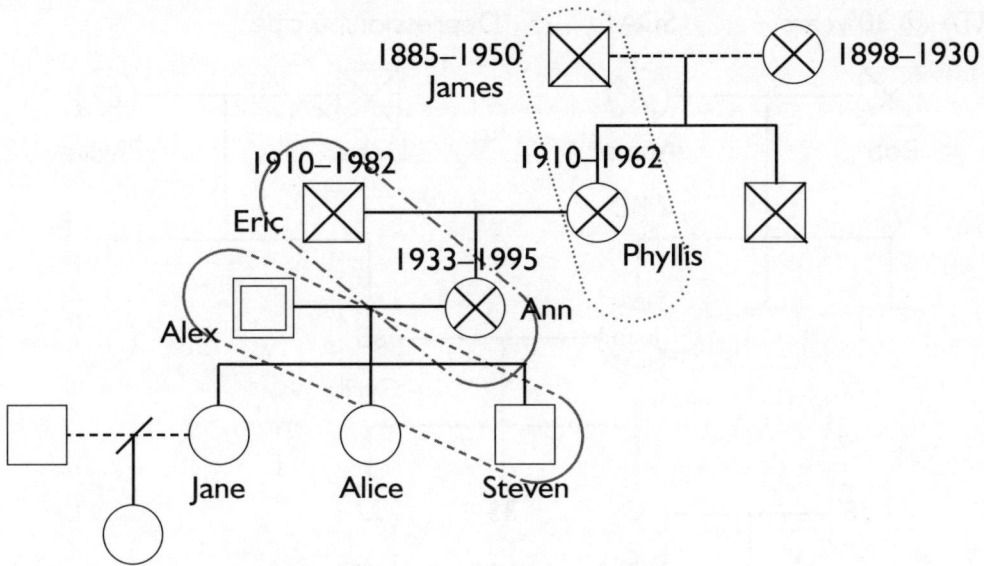

options for further support from health and social services. The clinical old-age psychiatry team had found Jane's concerns difficult to understand and were helped greatly by the use of a genogram. The genogram helped to identify the family tradition of female gendered caring and to address this directly with the family, for example establishing what the origins of their beliefs about caring were, and how this matter might be causing a dilemma for various family members. In this instance the use of the genogram to explore family themes and recurring patterns across the generations helped family members and clinicians to a greater understanding of the issues involved in the care of the elderly parent.

Specimen Genogram: Illness and the Family
A further common theme when working with elderly people and their families concerns illness within the family, particularly when specific types of illness have recurred within the family. Many families have particular anxieties about dementing illnesses and the following genogram portrays an example of a family where anxieties surrounding the care of elderly relatives with a diagnosis of dementia were a major issue for the family.

RTA @ 30 years   SDAT   Depression/Suicide

Bob   Annie   Derek   Phyllis (87)

MID

Joan — Cyril (65)

38 — Sylvia (35)   Susan (33)   Josie (27)
                    └─── Abroad ───┘

(4)   (3)

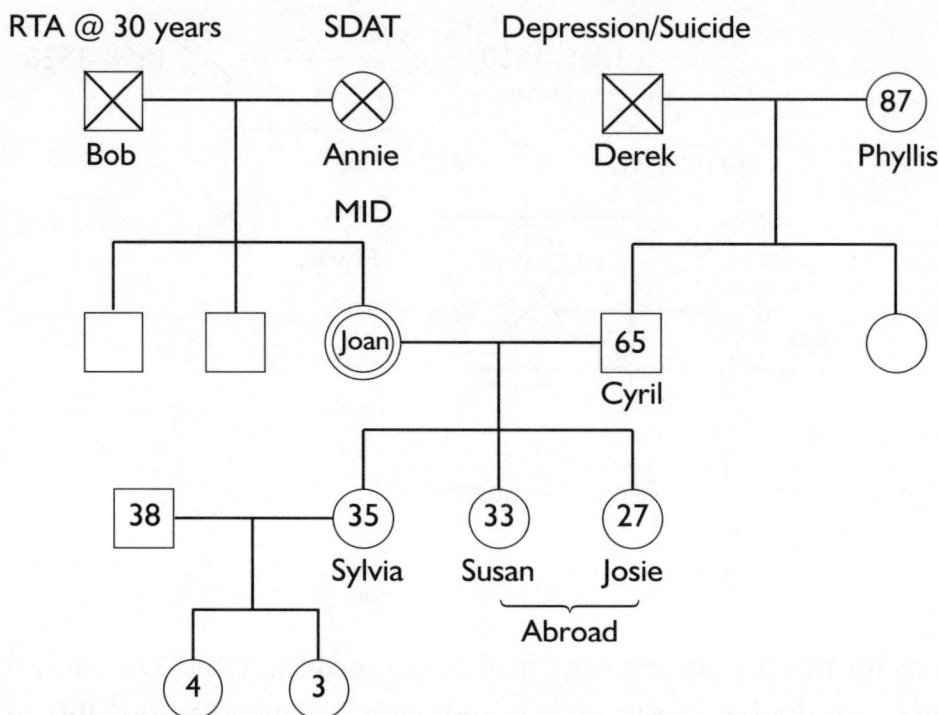

The referred person in this family is Joan, who was referred by her family doctor to an old-age psychiatry service for assessment, and was said to be forgetful and having difficulty expressing herself verbally. Assessment, including a neuropsychological assessment and CT brain scan, suggested a diagnosis of multi-infarct dementia. Sylvia, the eldest daughter, had repeatedly telephoned Joan's doctor and other services asking for urgent help to assist Cyril in caring for Joan. When the old-age psychiatry team met with family members and a genogram was drawn, various patterns and themes emerged.

Joan's mother, Annie had died following a long illness which had been diagnosed as Alzheimer's Disease, and Joan had been Annie's main carer during her illness. Annie had lived with Joan and Cyril for 12 months prior to her death. Annie's husband, Bob, died many years before this in a road traffic accident. When Joan herself became forgetful, Sylvia had assumed that Joan had the same illness as her mother, Annie, and this had raised anxieties about who would care for Joan and in what way. Sylvia had been particularly worried because Cyril had described feeling 'low' recently when contemplating the changes in his wife. Cyril was able to reflect, when drawing the parts of the genogram which related to his own parents, that his own father, Derek, had killed himself, aged 70, after a ten-year experience of depression, which followed his redundancy from work, aged 60. Cyril felt Sylvia had worried that he might become depressed like his father, especially as Cyril had himself retired from work in the past year. However Cyril felt his retirement would, on the contrary, help him, as he would have more time to care for Joan, which he wished to do. This example illustrates how recurring themes in the family, relating particularly to illness and death, were important to different family members' perception of their present situation, and their perception of what may help.

Other common examples of recurring patterns within late life families include situations where alcohol or drug abuse has recurred across generations, where roles such as being a carer or being 'the breadwinner' have been assigned to particular genders across generations, and where there has been a family history of mental health problems or suicide.

Exercise

1   Attempt to draw at least three generations of your family tree, using the genogram format outlined above, and to indicate the nature of the relationships between yourself and other family members, as you perceive them at the present time. Are there any recurring patterns or themes across the generations of your family?

2   Try asking a friend or colleague's permission to draw their genogram. Try interviewing them in order to gather information about at least three generations of their family and drawing their genogram as you go along.

3   Try to draw a family map including several generations of your family in relation to yourself. Indicate the nature of the relationships between individuals as you perceive them at the present time. Consider whether there are any 'hierarchies' in your family map, which would be indicated by the position of the person on the map.

You could try reviewing your family map in a few months' time. Do you still view the relationships in the same way? If not, what factors may have been important in changing your perception of them?

CHAPTER 3

HYPOTHESISING:
A way of developing ideas

THIS CHAPTER INTRODUCES HYPOTHESISING and how we may develop ideas about the elderly person and their family. It describes using hypotheses and testing them in order to structure an assessment of family need. The ideas are illustrated with a case example of an elderly person considering with his wife and son, whether to move into residential care, and introduces a practical exercise for the reader to identify hypotheses from the perspectives of the different family members, and from the perspective of the professional team working with the family.

A theory to be proved or disproved by reference to the facts.
A supposition made as a basis for reasoning without assumption of its truth.
A starting point for further investigation.
A provisional explanation of anything.

Standard dictionary definitions of hypotheses illustrate how they are seen to be a way of generating ideas about things, which provide a starting point from which we can travel further by way of investigation. Hypothesising has long been felt to be a crucial aspect of the scientific method, and the scientific method of investigation is often seen to have a number of stages, which include developing ideas and hypotheses about the phenomena we are interested in. When working with older adults and their families we may follow similar steps. We may *observe* the characteristics of our referred client and family, and we may share our observations by *describing* them to colleagues. We may then generate *hypotheses* or ideas about the family system based on our observations, and which we can seek to check out or *verify* by talking with the family and collecting further information about the family system.

However, there are also a number of ways in which our behaviour when working with families does not accord with the scientific method. The scientific method usually assumes that our observations will be valid, reliable and reproducible, whereas when working with families the situation is usually more fluid and dynamic than this. When working in the field of 'pure science' it is easier to develop clear descriptions of our area of investigation based upon our observations, as we are dealing with phenomena that are usually subject to fewer unexpected changes and which tend to respond in the same way when the same event comes into contact with them. Families are not like this. The family system may behave differently when faced with the same sorts of events because it is a complex phenomenon and over time interactions may differ in many ways. Rather than having one accurate observation of a family system, different observers may describe the same family in different ways and develop different hypotheses about them. Indeed this 'unscientific' process whereby colleagues working together in a team may make different observations and generate different hypotheses about the same family meeting is often a desirable consequence of working in teams with families. The process by which the family is able to listen to and share the team's different ideas about their situation can sometimes be a most important factor in generating change. If the family were only provided with one explanation it may fail to be helpful or may help only certain members of the family system.

In Chapter 4, the differences between *circular* and *linear* questions are outlined. Hypotheses are usually stated in linear terms when using the scientific method of investigation, for example, 'If ... then ...'. The proposition is that, if a specific event occurs then a specific result or outcome can reliably be expected to occur too. However, hypotheses about families are usually more complex than this. There are likely to be many variables that are important to the family system, and they are likely to produce different effects at different points in time. Families face many life events and changing circumstances, which may have specific effects upon individuals within the family but also have effects upon the family system as a whole. These effects may vary according to when the life event occurs in the history of the family life cycle, and depending upon other events which the family may be experiencing at the same time. Rather than developing linear hypotheses when working with families, we therefore need to develop *systemic* hypotheses (see below) which take more account of the complexities in families and the large number of events and issues which can impact upon the family system.

SYSTEMIC HYPOTHESISING

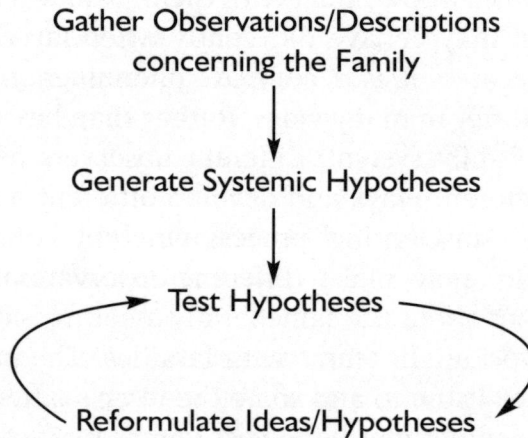

Gather Observations/Descriptions
concerning the Family

↓

Generate Systemic Hypotheses

↓

→ Test Hypotheses

Reformulate Ideas/Hypotheses

Gathering Observations/Descriptions Concerning the Family
This may involve using information from a wide range of sources, including information from the referring agent and information from other professionals and services. The clinician may also have information provided by the client and family prior to the family meeting and information about the social circumstances and environment within which the family is functioning.

Sometimes clinicians may worry about the amount of information available concerning a family. If clinicians feel they 'know too much' about a client or family members before a family meeting, because they have already met with the client or family members in a different context of the service, it may be helpful for OTHER members of the team to take on the role of interviewing and talking with the family when they attend for a meeting. This may allow new perspectives to be developed, while still taking advantage of the information which the clinician, who has the most prior knowledge of the family, can provide. It should be recognised that, in some circumstances, clinicians who have worked with a client prior to the family meeting may have developed a perspective which reflects the current system of the family, rather than a perspective which will allow change to occur. This is often referred to as the clinician becoming 'part of the family system', and can happen to any clinician, however experienced they may be in working with families. The important factor is often being able to recognise that this is occurring and that it may be influencing our perspective upon the family. This can be difficult, but our colleagues can sometimes help us to recognise when we are 'stuck' with the family system in this way. Sometimes a wealth of detail about the family can bring with it assumptions and expectations about the family system which may limit, as much as inform, the way we work. Consider this quotation from Dunham (1977) describing this phenomenon with respect to the scientist conducting a scientific investigation, 'Inevitably, the more a scientist knows about a problem the more assumptions he acquires about the nature of the world, thereby limiting his ability to discover new and different phenomena that are contrary to these assumptions.' (p4)

The converse situation occurs when clinicians feel they have too little information concerning the family. This may be most likely to occur when a written referral letter has been received from a referring agent, and none of the family members are already known to the service receiving the referral. Although this may generate anxiety in clinicians it is generally not as much of a problem as having 'too much' information, and can have a number of advantages. The clinician(s) who see the family will still be able to develop some ideas or hypotheses about the family prior to meeting with them, but will also be able to see the family with a relatively 'clean slate', which allows the first session to be an information gathering experience. Further hypotheses can be developed without the contamination of prior beliefs and assumptions concerning the family influencing the ability of the clinicians to think creatively about them.

Having less information *can* be helpful when a client has been known to a service for some time, and when various approaches have been tried culminating in an attempt to see the family as a whole. Family approaches are often considered in this situation, when many other attempts at seeing the elderly client for individual forms of intervention are perceived as having failed. If the family are seen in these more difficult circumstances it can often be more productive for the clinicians who meet with the family *not* to gather what is likely to be a large volume of available information about the client, but rather to try to look at things from a new perspective. This can often be an approach which the client and family appreciate too, as they are likely to have had a long experience of perceiving services as having failed to help the situation of their elderly relative and themselves in relation to this person. This may particularly apply to older people with long-standing physical or mental health problems who may have been in contact with services for many years. In this situation it can often be helpful to commence the family meeting by introducing a number of 'open' questions about the family situation. For example:

Who in your family wants to begin by telling us how things are for your family at present?

How do other family members see the situation at present?

What is your understanding as a family of why we are meeting today?

I have a little information about how things are for you as a family at present, but wondered if we could start by asking you to describe how you see the situation?

If the clinician commences the session by introducing the clinician's own understanding of the situation this is likely to be influenced by information which has been gathered in the past about the elderly client:

I understand that your mother has had difficulties in the past with depression, and that [...] have been tried. I wonder if you could tell us how you see the situation as a family.

I understand your difficulties are [...] at the moment, and that we are meeting together today to talk about them.

The clinician's opening remarks may set the scene for the conversation that follows and may increase the likelihood that themes which have already been addressed are repeated. In some circumstances this may be appropriate, but in others it may make it more difficult for the clinician to use the opportunity for a family meeting as an opportunity to introduce a different perspective on the situation.

Generating Systemic Hypotheses

Palazzoli Selvini *et al* (1980) define hypothesising in relation to families as 'the formulation by the therapist of an hypothesis based upon the information he possesses regarding the family he is interviewing'.

The clinician's hypotheses allow new ideas to be introduced to the family system which is important if the family are repeating strategies and sequences of behaviour which have not helped in the past and continue to fail to change the family system in the present. Systemic hypotheses are those which take account of the complex interactions in families and, as with circular questions they may be seen to generate ideas about the complex interactions in families. Systemic hypotheses suppose that the following model applies:

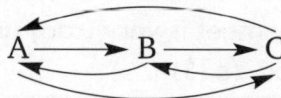

$$A \longrightarrow B \longrightarrow C$$

where A is presumed to have an effect upon B, which in turn has effects upon C, but that these effects also feed back and have effects upon A and B too.

One example of this may be that the clinician hypothesises that the elderly client's behaviour (A) has the effect of making her daughter visit more often (B), which in turn causes the husband and children of the daughter to become angry about the time the daughter is spending away from them (C). However the anger (C) may also be likely to have an effect upon the elderly parent's behaviour (A) and upon the daughter's perceptions of what visiting the elderly person achieves (B), which in turn may alter the sequence of events and behaviour. The clinician may generate systemic hypotheses in this way rather than in a more linear way. Linear hypothesising may have linked together the effects which the mother's behaviour had upon the daughter's visits and the other family member's expression of anger (that is, A B C), but which would be less likely to consider the implications of these links feeding back in a circular way into the family system and having additional implications of their own for that system.

It is important, when generating hypotheses, to think of as many possible explanations as we can concerning the family's functioning. Hypotheses which seem less likely to be helpful at the onset of work with the family may often prove to be helpful for several family members as work with the family progresses. Creative hypothesising, where more unusual or even 'off the wall' ideas are generated in a brainstorm session by the team concerning the family system, can often be very productive. This process allows the clinician(s), who meet the family, to develop a wider perspective upon the family, and increases the chance of introducing new ideas to them. However it is also important to introduce new ideas in such a way that the family are able to 'hear' them and accept them within their family system. Tom Anderson (1990) suggests:

> If people are exposed to the usual they tend to stay the same. If they meet something unusual, this unusual [sic] might induce a change. If the new they meet is very (too) unusual they close up in order not to be inspired. (p33)

Ways of using the ideas of team members creatively when working with families are considered further in Chapter 6 concerning reflecting teams, which covers the work of Tom Anderson and the Tromsø team in Norway in more detail.

Testing Hypotheses

Prior to meeting with a family, therefore, we may generate a range of ideas and hypotheses, either on our own or with the help of team members, based upon the information we have about the family. During the family meeting, we may test some of these ideas as part of the family interview. Information, which the family provide during the family meeting will also help us to generate further ideas and hypotheses about the family system. The process of checking our ideas or hypotheses in this way could be likened to a game of *Cluedo* or a good detective novel, where various possibilities are discounted by gathering evidence and information, until we reach the explanation which is most likely.

However, when thinking about hypotheses in relation to families, much current systemic thinking considers it more helpful to assume there are a number of possible ways in which families may be helped, and that there is unlikely to be one single 'answer', hypothesis or intervention which helps the family system. The process of a family meeting therefore involves a more complex investigation than the classic 'whodunit', which usually assumes there will be *one* solution to the mystery, rather than a range of possibilities, all of which may be helpful. This leads to the idea that, rather than thinking in terms of 'either/or' in relation to families, and assuming that either one hypothesis or one intervention rather than another may be helpful, it is more productive to think in terms of 'both/and'. This presumes that there are some possibilities which may help *and* there will be others too. Different ideas may be helpful for different family members. The role of the clinician is therefore not to find the 'answer' or single curative way of working with the family, but rather to help to generate a wider range of ways of viewing a family system. The process of talking with and exploring ideas and hypotheses with families is thought to be what generates the capacity in the family system for change, rather than a particular intervention which the clinician may suggest at the end of a treatment session.

It is also easier to be *creative* when trying to generate hypotheses if we are able to think in terms of several hypotheses being potentially useful for the family system, rather than imagining that our ideas will be *either* true *or* false. We may be less likely to contribute our ideas and hypotheses to a team discussion of a family, or to the family themselves, if we fear that our ideas may be 'wrong', and it may be more helpful to think in terms of several possible ways of helping the family system. It may also be helpful to remember that, even if one of our ideas or lines of inquiry does not seem to help the family system directly, it has nevertheless helped the information-gathering process, by helping us to understand that this particular idea is less useful to the family system than other ideas may be, and therefore it has helped us to better understand the family system. Palazzoli-Selvini *et al* described this, back in 1980: 'The hypothesis, as such, is neither true nor false, but rather more or less useful' (p5).

It is often also just as beneficial for families to develop an understanding of perspectives that are *not* helpful to them, as it is to know what *is* helpful. In 'real life', families will encounter a range of events and life experiences, some of which will have a positive effect and some of which will not. An understanding of both perspectives can be important.

Reformulating Ideas and Hypotheses

The information gathered when we meet the family will help to develop our hypotheses and will also allow us to develop further, new hypotheses about the family system. We may then check these hypotheses in further meetings with the family. Hypothesising is therefore a continuous process, and not just something which we do before interviewing the family for the first time.

When reformulating our ideas and hypotheses it is again important to be creative and flexible. We need to be aware of some of the pitfalls of developing favoured hypotheses, early in the course of seeing a family, or possibly prior to meeting with them, which we are then reluctant to shake off or change, even if the information provided by the family seems to suggest our original assumptions are not useful to the family system. If we stick with our original hypotheses in this inflexible and rigid way we are less likely to be able to help the family.

Cecchin (1987) has discussed how hypothesising and talking with families should be a lively process, where the effective clinician is someone who continues to generate new ideas and hypotheses about the family system, and who remains *curious* about the family system and its potential for change.

Using Questions to Generate Ideas and Hypotheses

We can generate ideas about family systems by thinking about various questions in relation to the family, many of which rely upon circular questioning techniques.

Some examples of questions which we may ask ourselves in relation to families in order to generate ideas are the following:

Why have the family presented now, rather than last month, six months or a year ago?

What are the consequences for the family/for each family member of the difficulties which they present now?

Do the presenting difficulties seem to have any function for the family or for family members?

What would be the advantages/disadvantages of change for the family or for individual family members?

Who in the family most/least wants change and why?

Who in the family most/least thinks there is a difficulty?

What important life cycle events seem to be occurring for the family and for individual family members?

Why have the family members who agree to attend the session decided to attend? How have those who decide not to attend reached their decision?

We can generate ideas by thinking about what we know of the family system as a whole, and we can also generate ideas by thinking about the situation from the perspective of individuals within the family system, or by thinking about our own role or the role of clinical services in relation to the family. The following case example and exercise illustrate how thinking about a family system from different perspectives can often help to generate new ideas about the family, and a greater appreciation of the situation they are facing.

Case Example

Arthur is a 76-year-old man who suffered a stroke some years ago and who has memory problems. He lives with his wife, Ellen, and son, Phillip, in Phillip's house. Ellen and Phillip have been frequently telephoning Arthur's family doctor and social services asking for something to be done to help them. They describe the main difficulty as 'wandering': Arthur leaves the house and does not say where he is going. However, on several occasions he has found his way to his sister's house, who lives nearby, but who Ellen and Phillip have not spoken to for many years, following a family dispute.

Phillip describes a feeling of tension in the house in the evening and describes how his father sits in silence, staring at the floor, and then suddenly gets up to leave. Phillip and Ellen have tried to prevent this by locking the doors and trying to persuade him not to go out, but this has not been effective. Ellen reports feeling worried that he may get lost or run over by a car, although he has always found his way back home to date. She is also worried about the future if Arthur's memory problems get worse, and has enquired whether Arthur alone, or both Arthur and herself, should move into residential care, as Phillip is planning to get married soon.

Arthur does not wish to live in residential care and does not feel there is a problem. Arthur's doctor arranged a short hospital assessment admission for him. Phillip initially refused to allow his father to return home, but later went to the ward and took him home without telling staff, and leaving his possessions on the ward.

Exercise

1   Try to place yourself in Arthur's position. Think about how you would feel in his situation and try to generate as many ideas and hypotheses as you can about his position.

2   Try to place yourself in Ellen and then Phillip's position and repeat the same exercise.

3   Try to place yourself in the position of 'the services' and consider what ideas and hypotheses the services may have about the situation.

CHAPTER 4

CIRCULAR QUESTIONS:
A way of interviewing

THIS CHAPTER DESCRIBES what circular questions are and how they differ from other forms of questioning used in the interview. The main categories of circular questions are introduced with examples. The chapter seeks to demonstrate how circular questions can be used in an interview as an information-gathering technique and to test hypotheses and ideas about the elderly person and their family. It discusses how circular questions can improve our understanding of relationships and interactions between family members, and concludes with an exercise which allows the reader to practise using circular questions by interviewing a colleague.

Questions in the Family Interview
Whenever the clinician puts a question to the client or family in the interview, the direction of the interviewing process will change to some degree. Even if the question is very open ended, such as 'How have you been since the last time we met?' or 'How do you see the situation at present?', it will set a context for what is to follow, and will direct the dialogue between clinician and client(s) in a particular way. Karl Tomm (1988) described this succinctly, 'To ask a particular question is to invite a particular answer.'

Questions in the interview can, of course, be framed in many different ways, and clinicians will seek information differently depending upon their personal style, their theoretical background and the type of information being sought. Questions in the assessment interview may be directed towards hypotheses which the clinician has about the family, but the responses to questions may, in themselves, generate further hypotheses for the clinician to explore. In many clinical interviews the client or family may be asked about presenting difficulties, and may be asked what they feel contributes to or, alternatively, helps the difficulties. They may be asked about the quality of their relationships with others and whether they feel this has any bearing upon the presenting difficulties. This allows the clinician to build up a picture of the nature of the presenting difficulties and the clients' perceptions. Linear, cause-and-effect, questions usually ask the client to specify outcomes in relation to some particular set of circumstances, as follows:

IF A ⟶ THEN B ⟶ THEN C

This form of questioning is often appropriately used, for example, by clinicians following a medical model, where the clinician seeks to clarify and explore causes of particular symptoms. A doctor attempting to understand the causes of an elderly person's back pain may ask the person to describe the pain (A), and may then ask what the person is restricted from doing as a result of the pain (B) and how much the restrictions affect the person's quality of life (C).

A future example of linear questions follows in this sequence of questions put to an elderly person presenting with symptoms of anxiety:

Question: What are your main difficulties at present?

Response: I get nervy and worry about things that didn't used to bother me in the past. (A)

Question: Can you think of an example of when you last felt nervous like that?

Response: It happened yesterday, when I thought about going out to the shops around the corner. My heart was beating fast and I felt sick. (B)

Question: Did how you felt stop you going out to the shops?

Response: Yes, it took a while for the feelings to die down, and I just sat and tried to watch the television instead. I didn't feel

> like trying to go out again, so my daughter did the
> shopping for me later. (C)

Linear questions tend to give us information about events and how they relate to one another, but they are a less effective way of understanding the complex interrelationships which exist in many family systems. In order to interview and converse with families in a way which avoids using only linear questions, we can generate questions and ideas which are 'circular', and more interactive. Circular questions can help us to explore and check our hypotheses with families. As described in the previous chapter, 'systemic hypotheses' try to take account of some of the complex relationships and interactions between family members, and circular questions are one way of further investigating our systemic hypotheses.

Rather than assuming that one event can cause another in a linear fashion, circular questions assume that the effects of any event also feed back in a circular fashion and have effects of their own. These effects may be upon the family but also upon the clinician and the questions which the clinician then chooses to ask next. Circular questions also assume that it is the *differences* between events or relationships which convey valuable information and that our understanding of something is limited if we view it on its own, but enhanced if we view it in relationship to something else. Advertisers of many products, from washing powder to pet food, exploit this in advertisements which seek to have us compare their product to something else. In everyday life we perpetually interpret the world around us in terms of reference to other things and to other contexts. For example, we may hold an item of clothing in a store up to the light in order to seek a different perspective on its colour before we buy it; and we may compare a piece of music we have not heard before with our experience of other pieces of music which we are more familiar with in order to help us to characterise or classify our appreciation of the new piece in some way.

Circular questions seek to bring out the differences between things. In terms of the family, circular questions seek to explore how individuals within the family relate to other individuals, and hence to develop an understanding of differences in relationships. However they also assume that, by seeking this sort of information, the situation or system will be changed as the very act of our posing or framing a question has some impact upon the family system and relationships. As with linear questions, circular questions are likely to have more value if they are asked in relation to ideas or hypotheses we may have about the family. This may involve exploring hypotheses already generated by the clinician, or we may use circular questions to generate more information, which allows the clinician to develop further hypotheses and ideas about the family system. In this sense the information collected when using circular questions feeds back ideas to the clinician and helps the clinician to develop further hypotheses which can be explored.

The major proponents of the use of circular questioning historically were the Milan systemic team of Palazzoli-Selvini and colleagues, and in one of their important papers they describe circularity as 'the capacity of the therapist to conduct his investigation on the basis of feedback from the family in response to the information he solicits about relationships and, therefore, about difference and change' (Palazzoli-Selvini *et al*, 1980).

In this same article the authors go on to describe the main types of circular questions. John Burnham (1986) went on to expand and clearly label categories of circular questions, and these are outlined below, with added examples, taken from interviews with elderly people and their families, where circular questions were used.

Categories of Circular Questions
1   Sequential questions
2   Action questions
3   Classification questions
4   Diachronic questions
5   Hypothetical questions
6   Mind-reading questions

Sequential Questions
These questions centre on what people actually *do* in particular interactions. A sequence of behavioural interactions would typically be the focus for enquiry, with the aim of understanding what occurs when

a particular set of circumstances arise. The clinician may explore what the key players in the interaction did, and how their actions related to one another.

An example of a dialogue follows in which a number of sequential questions are used to explore what happens when an elderly man with a dementing illness wanders from the house where he lives with his wife. Note how the clinician does not simply focus on asking each individual family member what they themselves did in the circumstances, but does focus on how people *related* to one another, and how family members perceive one another's behaviour and actions.

Son:	The problem is that my father wanders out of the house and gets lost.
Clinician:	What does your mother do when your father wanders out?
Son:	My mother gets really upset and tries to persuade him not to go out. She usually rings me if he manages to leave the house.
Wife:	If he isn't at home when I ring, I sometimes call the police because I'm so worried about what may happen to him.
Son:	Yes, she does, but then dad gets very worked up if he sees the police near the house.
Clinician:	What happens when you call your son, and he is at home?
Wife:	He comes to the house as soon as he can, even if it is the middle of the night, but he often can't persuade his dad not to go out either.
Clinician:	What happens then?
Wife:	He often gets angry with his dad and shouts at him, and then his dad gets worked up as well. If they're outside and shouting, the neighbours come out and complain and sometimes they call the police. Once his dad is that worked up, we can't get him inside for hours.

Action Questions

These questions attempt to enlarge upon statements which describe individuals in terms of intrinsic character traits, such as 'He's always been unable to cope', 'She's always been inadequate' or 'He is insensitive about things', and to enquire instead into the specific circumstances which have earned the person a particular label.

Daughter: My father has always been inadequate and has never been able to cope.

Clinician: What does your father do which makes you say he can't cope?

Daughter: Well, one example would be how he uses the telephone. He calls me all the time, and says he doesn't like being in the house on his own.

This short sequence of communication moves the clinician away from a fixed statement ('My father has always been inadequate'), which seems to suggest little hope for change from the daughter's perspective, to examples of what the focus of the elderly father's anxieties may be. The clinician can then go on to explore these further.

This form of question therefore seeks to challenge fixed statements which allow little room for change if taken at face value. By enquiring into the reasons for the statement, the clinician seeks to explore the statement in more detail, and to understand the circumstances which give rise to it. This often in turn allows further hypotheses about the situation to be developed.

Classification Questions

These questions explore how family members respond or react to particular interactions or situations, and try to classify or rank how individual members of the family see different things. The clinician may, for example, explore and classify how strongly beliefs or views are held by various family members, and also explore how different members of the family may be responding to the situation in different ways. This may also reveal that different members of the family have different perceptions about one another's position, and discussion of this in a family meeting can help to clarify issues. For example, 'I didn't realise you thought mother may be able to manage living alone, I thought you very strongly felt she should go into a home.' Classification questions may therefore challenge some of the inaccurate beliefs which members of the family hold about other family members, and which may be preventing change from occurring. The following conversation introduces a number of classification questions.

Clinician:	Who, in your family, do you think has been most affected by your retirement?
Father:	I think my wife has been more affected than me. She isn't used to having me under her feet all day and interfering with the things she's always done on her own.
Mother:	Yes, it has affected me more than I thought it would, but I still think it's affected me less than my husband. He never used to sit around all the time doing nothing. Even at the weekend, he was always busy.
Clinician:	After yourselves, has anyone else in the family been affected by the retirement?
Father:	Well, we see more of my son and grandchildren than we used to do, but I don't know if they always find that a good thing.
Clinician:	If your son was here, who do you think he would say was most affected by the retirement?
Father:	Me, definitely.
Mother:	I agree.

Diachronic Questions
These questions enquire into changes in behaviour which indicate a change in relationships before and after a specific event. Diachronic questions are particularly helpful when the family have difficulties which seem to relate to a change or transitional life event, and seem to be having difficulties adapting to the changes which have occurred as a result of that event.

Later life tends to be a stage of the life cycle in which people experience many transitional events, such as changes in physical health, hospital admissions, retirement and loss of partner or friends through death. Diachronic questions can therefore be particularly useful with older adults and their families. Following on from the example above, diachronic questions which the clinician may ask in relation to the effects of the retirement are as follows.

Clinician: You said you are spending more time with your son and grand-children. Has that changed since the retirement, or had you already started to see more of them beforehand?

Or:

Clinician: Are there any other ways in which you have done things differently as a couple since the retirement?

Hypothetical Questions

These questions explore how things would be different if particular hypothetical circumstances were to occur. They may explore differences of opinion in the family with respect to hypothetical situations if they had occurred at some time in the past, present or future. As the family are being asked to think hypothetically, they may find it easier and less threatening to generate ideas within the family as to how things could be different. This can be particularly helpful when families (and clinicians) are finding the realities of the present situation, and discussion of solutions which have already been tried, constraining and not productive of change. In the following example the clinician explores how the family feel the elderly mother's depression, and the family situation, could be different if particular circumstances in their lives were (hypothetically) different.

Clinician: You said that you have never known a time when Charlotte has not been depressed, or at least that you can't remember what it was like because the situation has been the same for so long. If Charlotte was not depressed, how do you think things could be different for your family at the moment? (*Present*)

Annabel: I think things would be completely different for everyone in the family, for me, my brother and my mum.

Peter: I agree with Annabel. We would all be less worried and would probably be leading much more independent lives than we are now.

Or:

Clinician: If Charlotte's depression had not gone on for as long as it has, do you think your lives would have been different over the years? (*Past*)

Peter: If she had not been depressed when I was younger I would probably have left home years ago.

Annabel: Yes, we would both probably be married and my mother would be a grandmother by now.

Charlotte: That would have been nice. I have always regretted that my children have not been able to lead a more independent life, and that I've never had many friends of my own age. I've never really needed to make friends, with my children always keeping me company.

Clinician: If you were able to make friends in the future with people of your age, do you think that would have any effect on your depression? (*Future*)

Charlotte: I'm sure it would, but I would need help to meet people. I don't have the confidence to introduce myself to people on my own.

Mind-Reading Questions

These questions explore the extent to which different family members are aware of each other's beliefs and thoughts about a situation, and what their perception of other people's beliefs is. It may also bring out different views within the family about important issues. One of the examples given above in the section concerning classification questions was both a classification *and* a mind-reading question: 'If your son was here, who do you think he would say was most affected by the retirement?' Other examples of mind-reading questions are as follows.

> *Clinician:* If your daughter had answered that question, what do you think she would have said?
>
> *Clinician:* If your grandmother was alive and could be with us today, do you think she would agree with what has just been said, or not?

Mind-reading questions can be usefully employed if a member of the family is finding it difficult to respond to a particular point, and could be asked the questions instead.

> *Clinician:* It seems like you are finding it difficult to respond to this. I wonder what you think your sister would say or think about it if she were asked the same thing?

Or:

> What do you think other family members would say in response to that question? Which of those views are most like/unlike your own views? (Classification Question)

When working with an elderly person with dementia, who is finding it difficult to express a view, it can often be helpful to ask if another member of the family could comment on what they feel their relative would wish to say if they were able. This can be a very effective way of preventing the perspective of the elderly person with dementia being overlooked in the family meeting, but the clinician would need to remain aware that the views expressed remain another family member's perception of the older person's view, rather than necessarily being a factual account of what the older person would actually have said themselves. Sometimes, if a family member has been able to express a view on behalf of the older person in this way, the person with dementia is able to indicate whether or not they share that same view, although they were unable to express it in such a complex way themselves; and this can be an important contribution to the family meeting.

A further technique which can be used within family meetings involves leaving an *empty chair* in the room to represent someone who is not present, but who is felt to be important to the family system. Mind-reading questions may be used in association with the use of an empty chair, for example:

Clinician: If your father could be present and was sitting in this chair next to us now, what do you think he would say?

This *structural move* can add weight to the question asked and help to focus the family's attention on the perspective of the missing person more effectively.

Applying Circular Questions

Circular questions can be used with varying numbers of people present in the therapeutic situation. It is possible to use circular questions when only *one* individual is present, and this is often a helpful way to explore beliefs which the individual client holds about relationships, and their relationship with others.

An example of a *mind-reading* question which could be used in this situation is: 'If your father were still alive, and could be here with us today, what do you think he would advise us to do?'

However circular questions are often used in relation to *triads*, where three family members are present and one person in the triad is asked to comment on the relationship between the other two people present. Peggy Penn (1982) has referred to this as 'gossiping in the presence' of others, as it involves the individual expressing a view about others in circumstances which allow the 'gossiping' to be heard by them. This could then be balanced as the other two people present could each, in turn, be asked to give a view about the relationship of the other two family members who are present from their own, different perspective.

Circular questions are often used to check the beliefs of those family members present, gradually involving more of them in the interview process. As seen above, circular questions can also be used to involve the wider family system as they can be used to gather information about the beliefs which those present have about those who are not in attendance.

Circular Questions and the Clinical Team

Circular questions can, therefore, be used in various ways to aid the clinician working directly with a family but they can also be used as a tool for assessing the beliefs and objectives of the clinical team. They can provide an effective way for the individual clinician or clinical team to reflect upon the assessment or therapeutic process, without the family.

Whilst members of families may often express varying and conflicting views about issues which are commonly encountered in services for older adults (for example, views about whether or not an elderly person wishes to leave their home and move to live in residential care) it should be recognised that various members of a professional team may also have disparate views about this kind of situation, even if these views are not explicitly expressed. It may be helpful for the team to openly reflect upon issues such as these using circular question techniques. The team considering the issue of residential care for an elderly client currently thought to be at risk at home may, for example, consider the following:

What does the team currently do when the person has difficulties at home? (Sequential Question)

What exactly is it about the elderly person's behaviour which has meant they have been labelled as being 'at risk' ? (Action Question)

Who would be most/least affected positively and negatively if the person moved into residential care; taking into consideration the position of the client themselves, other family members, members of the clinical team, staff and residents of the residential care home? (Classification Question)

How are relationships between the client and their family and the team likely to change if the client moves to residential care? (Diachronic Question)

If the elderly client does/does not go to live in residential care what do the team think the situation will be like in six months' time? (Hypothetical Question)

If the elderly person did not have dementia and were able to express a view, what does the team feel that view would be, and how strongly would it be held? (Mind-Reading Question)

This use of circular questioning within the team often helps to clarify beliefs of team members and can often help to disentangle the views of professionals from those of the client/family. This can be helpful in ensuring that therapeutic outcomes are achieved in relation to the needs of the client and family rather than those of ourselves. It may be helpful for the team to explore their views using circular questions in this way whenever there is a difficulty because the views of the team and the views of the client or family seem to conflict, as when, for example, the elderly client refuses an offer of hospital admission, or does not comply with a form of treatment which the team feel will be beneficial.

Circular questions can also be used to help team members to reflect upon situations where they feel 'stuck' with a particular client's situation. Just as family members may refer to individual relatives as having intrinsic fixed characteristics when they feel frustrated about a lack of progress, team members may do the same. Clinicians, in this situation, may often reflect that a family or client is 'impossible' or 'difficult', and this may become a self-fulfilling prophecy, which restricts future ideas and change. Accepting statements such as these at face value may well have implications for the therapeutic approach and range of treatment opportunities offered to the client, and it may therefore be important to explore them further.

John O'Brien (1981) has addressed the issue of how negative expectations can influence outcome when working with people with learning disabilities. Applying his model to the above example may produce the outcome as outlined below:

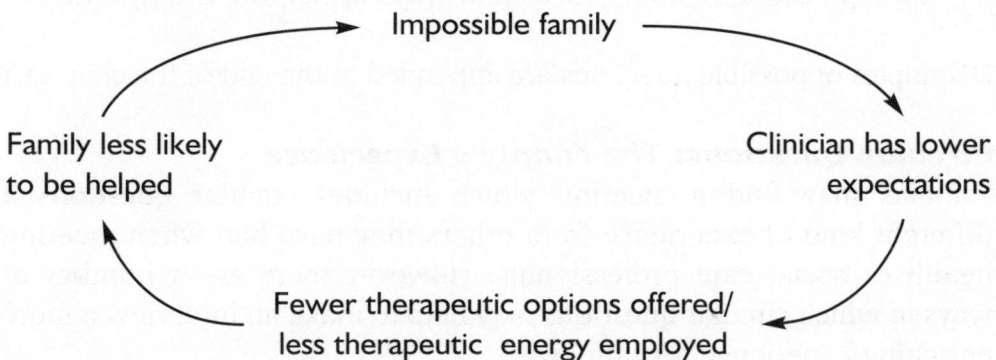

Impossible family

Family less likely to be helped

Clinician has lower expectations

Fewer therapeutic options offered/ less therapeutic energy employed

The team may find it helpful to use *action questions* to reflect upon what it is about the family presentation, situation or behaviour which has earned the label of 'impossible family', and could use circular questions as follows:

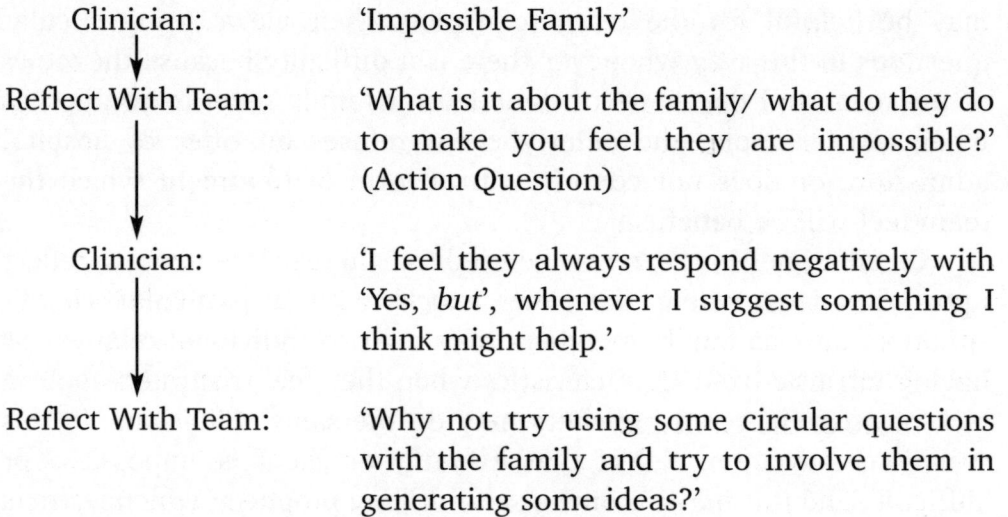

Clinician:	'Impossible Family'
	↓
Reflect With Team:	'What is it about the family/ what do they do to make you feel they are impossible?' (Action Question)
	↓
Clinician:	'I feel they always respond negatively with 'Yes, *but*', whenever I suggest something I think might help.'
	↓
Reflect With Team:	'Why not try using some circular questions with the family and try to involve them in generating some ideas?'

Exercise

1   Try to generate at least one example of each type of circular question which may help the clinician who feels stuck with this family.
2   Go back to the descriptions and examples of circular questions listed earlier in the chapter.
3   Try to think of questions which will help to involve the family more in thinking about ideas and ways of helping the situation.

(Examples of possible questions are appended at the end of the chapter.)

Circular Questions: The Family's Experience

Families may find a meeting which includes circular questions a different kind of experience from others they have had when meeting health or social care professionals. However there are a number of ways in which circular questions may help to make an interview a more enriching experience for families.

1   Families may enjoy the opportunity to provide their own perspective. The therapist is seeking the views of the family, rather than providing an interpretation only from the therapist's point of view.

2   Circular questions allow family members to explore how other people in the family view the same situation, and to explore the differences in perspectives within the family.

3   Circular questions help the family to generate their own ideas and solutions to difficulties. Discussions about different points of view and an understanding of how other members of the family view one another can help towards an understanding of the difficulties for the family themselves.

4   Many standard hospital appointments leave the client telling their family about 'what the doctor asked', whereas circular questions help to focus the family discussion on how change can occur, and how the family's ideas about this are usually more important than those of the clinician.

'A good circular interview will leave the family remembering the answers they gave rather than the questions they were asked.' (Street & Dryden, 1988, p62)

Examples of Circular Questions
Examples of circular questions which help resolve the clinician's dilemma are given below.

Sequential Questions
Can each member of the family describe what they do at the moment when faced with the present difficulty?
What solutions have the family already tried?
Who did what in the family when trying to find their own solutions?
Can each family member suggest something that they could *do* differently which they think may help the family situation?

Action Questions
The clinician reflects that they seem to be finding it difficult to think of ways to help the family with change and asks if any of the family can help to think of ideas which will help the clinician to move things on.

Classification Questions
Who most thinks things can change/who most thinks they can't?
Who will be most/least affected if things change/do not change?

Diachronic Questions
Who in the family was closer/less close before the present difficulties arose? Who in the family saw more/less of each other before the difficulties arose?

Hypothetical Questions
What do the family think things will be like for each member of the family if the situation has not changed in six months or a year's time? How do the family think things will be for each member if they no longer have their current difficulties in six months or a year's time?

Mind-Reading Questions
The clinician could ask the family whether there is anybody not present at the family meeting who might have a view about how things might be different, or could ask what the family imagine other families might say/do if they were faced with the same situation.

CHAPTER 5

THE FAMILY LIFE CYCLE:
A way of understanding

THIS CHAPTER INTRODUCES the concept of the family life cycle, and considers events and issues which are found in its later stages. It discusses how a consideration of life cycle issues may help us to understand the needs of elderly people and their families from a different perspective, and how life cycle events may sometimes conflict for different members of the family, and influence their capacity to offer support to the elderly person. The chapter includes case examples which invite the reader to identify late life cycle issues and to consider a care-giving situation from the standpoint of several different family members, each with their own perspective.

Life Cycle Models
As we age we pass through different stages of development and encounter various life events. Life cycle models of development are only one example of many attempts to categorise or divide periods of human development into stages, and there are a number of accounts of individual development. Family life cycle models try to incorporate the developmental cycle across the history and development of a *family*, and one of the most well known accounts of family life cycle stages is that of Carter and McGoldrick (1989). They describe six stages of the family life cycle, which advance development of the family:

1   Leaving home: single young adults
2   The joining of families through marriage: the young couple

3   Families with young children
4   Families with adolescents
5   Launching children and moving on
6   Families in later life

The authors also describe some of the emotional effects of these life cycle stages, and the developmental changes needed to progress through each developmental stage. Many individuals within families do not, of course, necessarily experience or aspire to all of these life cycle stages, and may not, for example, marry or have a partner, may not have children and may never leave the parental home. Issues relating to sexuality, gender and ethnicity will also have a considerable impact upon the experiences of individuals within families, and their experience of life cycle changes in relation to the family. However experiencing the late life stage of the life cycle is something which most people aspire to, and yet, at the same time, sometimes dread, because of the negative consequences which are often associated with later life.

There are other models of the family life cycle which also divide different aspects of the life cycle into developmental stages or periods. Hughes *et al* (1978), for example, divide the life cycle into seven stages, the last stage of which concerns retirement and ageing. Barnhill and Longo (1978) divide the life cycle into nine transitional periods, the ninth of which deals with retirement and 'old age'. Barnhill and Longo view the life cycle from a psychoanalytic perspective and suggest that difficulties and problems in families can arise when the life cycle does not progress smoothly through the transitional stages of development. Although the various models of the family life cycle have different theoretical perspectives, they tend to have in common a perspective which emphasises the earlier years of the life cycle at the expense of the late life period. The earlier chronological years of life are often portrayed as being much more 'developmentally active' than the later and post-retirement years. All of the models outlined above devote only one of their stages to later life and the years after retirement, when this time period may span almost as many years as the other stages added together.

When we examine the later years of the family life cycle, a number of developmental events are evident which, although not biologically productive in the sense of producing children, are developmentally productive and important to family life. The following case example illustrates a number of the developmental challenges of later life families, and you may wish to identify them as you read the case example.

Case Example

Agnes is 89 years old and worries about her failing eyesight and reduced mobility. More recently she has been feeling low in mood, following the death of her sister-in-law, who was her husband's youngest sister. She is now the only survivor of her generation in the family, as her own siblings died some years ago. Agnes husband died five years ago, and she now lives with her daughter, Molly, and son-in-law, Harold. Molly is 64 years old and Harold recently retired from his job as a printer after working with the same firm for 47 years. Molly and Harold had been looking forward to his retirement and have plans for things they would like to do, including travelling more often abroad together. Agnes has three grandchildren, one of whom lives nearby, eight great-grandchildren, and also has a great-great-granddaughter, aged two years. She enjoys visits from younger members of the family.

This brief description of Agnes and her family identifies a number of developmental experiences of later life.

Agnes is experiencing *grandparenthood, great-grandparenthood, and great-great-grandparenthood, loss of a partner and siblings* through death, and is experiencing *changes in health* and well-being.

Molly and Harold are also experiencing common later life-cycle events such as *retirement* from paid work, *grandparenthood* and *great-grandparenthood*. they are also experiencing *caring for an elderly parent*, which, as the population ages, is increasingly becoming an experience of older adults themselves.

In addition to these life events, they may also be undergoing a number of adjustments, which are less overt, but nevertheless very important to the development of older individuals within families. Agnes, for example, may be adapting to the following:

◆   the experience of seeing her own children age

◆ the experience of nearing the end of her life and preparing for death

◆ the experience of being offered care, or having dependency needs met by younger members of the family

◆ the experience of seeing her family develop and continue to reproduce across several generations

◆ the experience of being the last remaining survivor of her generation in the family.

The life cycle and the roles which various members of the family adopt at different stages of the life cycle may be perceived very differently by different families. There may, for example, be different views across families as to what is an appropriate role for adult children when older parents have high dependency needs. Some families would feel adult children had an important role to play in caring for a frail older parent, whereas other families may not share this view. Contrast this statement by an elderly women with a dementing illness, directed at her son: 'I don't want you to give up your life to look after me. You have to think of your own family', with this statement from a daughter contemplating her mother's disabilities: 'I would give up my chances of marriage and having a happy life for now to care for my mother, if it would make her happy.'

These two individuals were not from the same family, but sometimes within a family, different generations may not share the same expectations and beliefs about caring for older family members, and distress and conflict can be the result. Some years ago, Blenkner (1965) suggested that one of the roles which may emerge when older parents have dependency needs is a role which requires *filial maturity*. Here, the adult child develops a filial role which incorporates some responsibility for the care of a parent, and this may be viewed by the adult child as an expected stage of their life cycle development. However, within other families this filial role is not expected. This role is not the same as a *reversal of roles,* where the older parent and adult child are seen to 'reverse' the role of caring in their relationship, such that the parent, who was in an earlier developmental stage the carer of the child, becomes the *receiver* of care from the adult child. A role requiring filial maturity assumes that the adult child takes on a caring role to help the older person to meet dependency needs, but that they nevertheless *maintain* their roles and position as parent and child in the family.

There are other examples of ways in which different individuals within the same family may have conflicting or different views about events associated with the later stages of the life cycle. The partner of a retiring adult may, for example, have plans for retirement which include their spending more time together, developing new social activities and interests, and spending a retirement lump sum; whereas the retiring person may fear a loss of activity, a loss of social contact with work colleagues and loss of income, and may worry about spending more time with their partner. Younger family members may look forward to a parent's retirement, hoping it will allow the parent to have more time to spend with grandchildren, but this may not accord with the older adult's hopes for retirement, if an increase in babysitting duties is not on the agenda! Many families adjust successfully to the demands of later life cycle events and work through differences in viewpoint and expectations in the family. Other families do not. As Froma Walsh (1989) points out: 'The salient transitions and tasks of later life hold potential for loss and dysfunction, but also for transformation and growth' (p312).

When encountering events associated with the later stages of the life cycle, the family system will inevitably change. Usually a new balance will be achieved within the family with respect to the way individual family members interact with one another, but sometimes families may have difficulties with adaptation. The following case example concerns a family where the family system which had operated successfully for many years was no longer able to function successfully, following a common late life-cycle event, the death of a partner.

Case Example

James and Sonya had eight children, all of whom lived within 10 miles of them, and all of whom were married with children of their own. They regarded themselves as a close family, who communicated regularly, and often organised social events and activities involving several members of the family. About 18 months after Sonya died, James presented with anxiety symptoms and feelings of low mood to the mental health service, and one of his concerns was that his family had changed since the death of his wife and that he no longer felt 'in touch' with his children and grandchildren. A family interview, which most of the children attended, revealed that Sonya had always played a pivotal role in communication between members of the family. She often acted as a 'switchboard' relaying messages and plans to her large family, who were in frequent contact with her. James would often carry through and participate in the arrangements which Sonya had made, including fishing trips or going to the football match with his children, and other social events. After Sonya's death the family had experienced a period in which they did not feel like continuing similar activities as they grieved for Sonya's loss, and later no-one in the family took over the role of Sonya as communications link for the large family. Indeed, until the family met as a family with the service, they had not openly identified how difficult it had been for them to communicate arrangements and coordinate a timetable in a large family. Having identified the importance of this role within the family, it became easier for them to decide how to proceed, and two of the children began to develop this role of communicator and organiser within the family.

Part of the explanation for different perceptions within the family is that the life cycle is a changing, evolving phenomenon, with different family members at different stages at different points in time. Sometimes the need for closeness or distance in relationships between family members will complement one another and allow needs to be met, but at other times needs within relationships will be different and there will be what Walsh (1989, p324) calls a 'lack of complementarity or fit'.

The Family Life Spiral Model

Another way to describe differences in perspective between different family members is with reference to the ideas of Combrinck-Graham (1985) and the life spiral model. This suggests that there will be some family life experiences and tasks which are assisted if the family members operate more closely to one another, and others which require the family members to establish a greater distance between them. One example of an event where the family may be helped by 'closeness' between individual members concerns the birth of a child, where the new parents may be assisted and supported by other family members, both practically and emotionally. However, when young adults leave the family home to live elsewhere, they may feel the need for a period of greater emotional and geographical 'distance' from other family members.

Combrinck-Graham refers to *centripetal* forces which operate during periods of family closeness and *centrifugal* forces, which operate to maintain distance. Problems may arise if family members' needs conflict. An elderly person, for example, may have dependency needs following a period of ill-health, and would benefit most from closer contact and support from other family members ('centripetal' needs), whereas the person in the family who may be identified as the main 'supporter', may themselves have needs which require some distance from this close relationship ('centrifugal' needs), such as concentrating on a new job or establishing a new personal relationship outside the family of origin. In this situation each family member is at a different stage of the life cycle, and has different needs, which do not complement one another.

The following case example illustrates this further.

Case Example

Ellen is a 72 year old woman referred by her family doctor to the old-age psychiatrist with depression. On assessment, she describes a number of depressive symptoms and, as she also expresses thoughts of self harm, is admitted to a psychiatric ward for further assessment. Within a few days of admission she begins to report feeling much better and is less troubled by depressive symptoms.

When at home, Ellen lives with her daughter, Linda, who is 41 years old. Linda has spent most of her time at the hospital since her mother's admission and has taken time off from her job at a bank in order to do this. She has lived with her parents for most of her life, and describes herself as her mother's 'sole companion' since the death of her father several years ago. Linda has recently developed her first serious personal relationship, and has been contemplating moving out from her mother's house to live with her partner. She expresses the view that her mother's illness is directly related to this.

In this case example Linda appears to be meeting many of Ellen's needs for companionship, following the death of Ellen's husband. Their relationship has been close for many years, and this 'centripetal' phase has been satisfactory for both of them. When Linda developed a new personal relationship she entered a 'centrifugal' phase and began to need to establish some distance from her mother, whilst Ellen's needs for closeness remained. This change in the family system was seen to be a major factor in precipitating Ellen's feelings of low mood. At the age of 41, Linda is considering 'leaving home' at a later chronological age than is common in terms of the life cycle. If she had decided to leave home earlier in the life cycle of the family, her needs for some relative distance might have complemented her parent's needs more closely. For example, her father might have still been alive, and Ellen and her husband might have met one another's needs for closeness, as well as providing one another with companionship, and been able to adjust more readily to the challenge of an 'empty nest'.

It has been argued that there may be particular problems for family systems when life cycle events do not progress 'as expected', and there are a number of other examples of this which may occur in the later stages of the life cycle and have a considerable impact upon older adults and other family members.

Death of an Adult Child
The death of an adult child which occurs before the death of an ageing parent or parents, as with the death of a younger child within the

family, is often an unexpected and unprepared for life event. This can have obvious psychological effects in the period after the death as the older parent grieves for the loss of their child. However the death of an adult or middle-aged child may also have more enduring psychological and practical effects. The older adult may already have been receiving care from the adult child or may have had expectations that the adult child would help to support any possible care needs if necessary in the future. Any surviving siblings may need to prepare themselves for a different role with respect to ageing parents than might have been the case had their sibling survived, and caring for an elderly parent without a deceased sibling's expected help may have important psychological and practical implications for caring. The older parent may themselves have lost the opportunity to experience the role of grandparent if the child died without having children of their own, and may mourn this loss, as well as grieving for the well-established relationship which they may have had with their adult child.

Remarriage in Later Life

When an elderly parent remarries later in life, the older adult and/or their children may be concerned about how other family members will respond. This may relate to feelings about personal relationships or feelings about sexuality and ageing. The elderly parent or children may feel concerned about how the remarriage will make them feel about the memory of their deceased parent in situations where remarriage follows a period of widow/widowerhood. The children may have concerns about adjusting to a new stepfamily. This may also be a concern for families where remarriage occurs at an earlier stage of the life cycle between two younger people, but in later life the step-family may encompass several more generations. Children may inherit quite a large step-family including not only stepsiblings, but also step-nieces/nephews and their offspring too.

To experience the family life cycle, then, is to experience the phenomenon of continuing change, which requires development and adjustment on the part of families. Often multiple roles are involved because, as we change, and perhaps experience the roles of parent, grandparent and great-grandparent, we may still be experiencing being a daughter/son or granddaughter/grandson, and our own experiences in these roles will give us expectations about how other family members may fulfil these roles too. Chapter 7 of the book addresses the important issue of our own expectations and experiences of family life more fully, but it seems important to remember that, although similar family life cycle events tend to be encountered across different families, there is no 'typical' picture of the family facing retirement, bereavement and other later life cycle issues. Families will meet each of these challenges in their own ways.

CHAPTER 6

REFLECTING TEAMS:
A way of working with colleagues

THIS CHAPTER INTRODUCES the concept of working as a 'reflecting team'. It describes how we may draw upon the ideas of colleagues when assessing and working with the elderly person and their family. It also considers different ways in which reflecting teams may be helpful in clinical practice, both when working with families and when working with colleagues in teams.

Working with Colleagues

Whilst many clinicians working with families work alone, there can be a number of advantages to working with others as a team. There are various ways in which the skills and experiences of professional colleagues can be drawn upon when working together, one of which is described in Chapter 1. One way of thinking which has had a considerable impact upon clinical practice in the field of family therapy in recent years centres around the ideas developed by Tom Anderson and the Tromsø team in Norway, concerning the reflecting team.

When working together, different individuals within the team may have different ideas about a family, and yet, in most traditional models of family therapy, only one position or message is usually conveyed to the family. The team may feel some pressure to reach a consensus in this situation, and it may mean that the family never hear many of the interesting ideas and different perspectives which different team members may have held. Working as a reflecting team addresses this, as it allows different viewpoints to be conveyed to the family and to the clinician who is talking with the family. Rather than conveying messages or ideas to the clinician who meets the family via a telephone or other communication system, which does not allow the family to hear the communication directly, a reflecting team approach allows a more 'open' system to operate as the team reflect their ideas to the family directly.

The Reflecting Team

Anderson describes how his Tromsø team first used the idea of working as a reflecting team when they were working in a more traditional way, with a family and clinician in one room and the remaining members of the team in another listening to and watching the family meeting using a sound and vision link. However, on this occasion, the team decided to give the family and interviewing clinician the option of hearing and seeing the team reflecting about the session and they did this by turning around the sound and vision system, so that the family and interviewing clinician could observe the team, rather than vice versa. Hence the clinician and family were able to hear a range of views and different perspectives presented by the team, without the need for the team to reach any consensus view about the family system. The sound and vision system was then restored to the original position and the interviewing clinician and family could themselves reflect upon the ideas they had heard expressed by the team.

One way of working using the ideas concerning reflecting teams would be as follows:

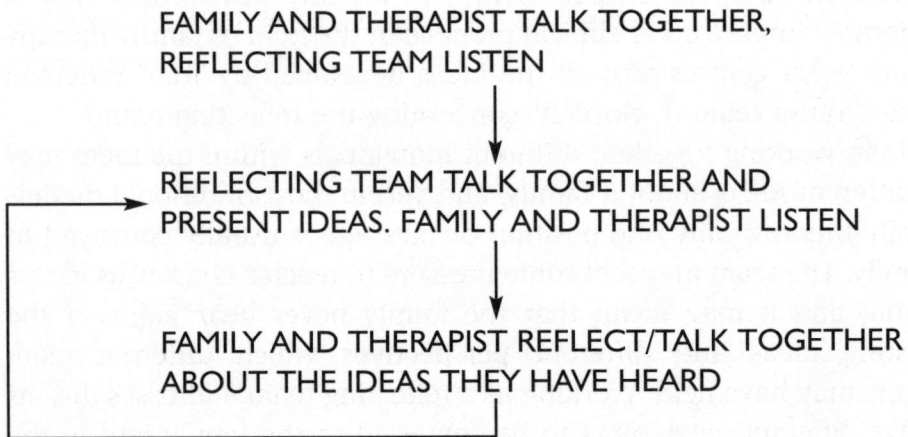

FAMILY AND THERAPIST TALK TOGETHER,
REFLECTING TEAM LISTEN

↓

REFLECTING TEAM TALK TOGETHER AND
PRESENT IDEAS. FAMILY AND THERAPIST LISTEN

↓

FAMILY AND THERAPIST REFLECT/TALK TOGETHER
ABOUT THE IDEAS THEY HAVE HEARD

The team may reflect their ideas to the therapist/family on only one occasion during a family meeting, or on several occasions if the family and interviewing therapist find this helpful. Anderson discusses how the word 'reflecting' in this context is from the French or Norwegian, meaning that 'something heard is taken in and thought about before a response is given' (1990, p.28).

The issue of having time and space to think about what a family is saying is an important one. When a lone therapist is interviewing a family with several members it can be difficult to attend to all of the content of the session and also to think about the issues presented by the family. The therapist may be concentrating on asking questions and responding to the content of the family conversation rather than 'listening' to the family. In many traditional uses of a back-up team where the team sit in a different room to the interviewing clinician and the family, it may also be difficult for team members to 'listen' to what the family say, and attend to all of the issues, because the back-up team usually engage in a dialogue about what the family are saying during the session: they may be discussing these issues while the family and therapist continue to speak, and may therefore miss important information. When working as a reflecting team, however, Anderson suggests that the team should not engage in a dialogue about the issues. Instead, they should listen quietly to the family and interviewing clinician, only reflecting their ideas directly when the family and clinician are listening. Anderson sees the role of the team as listening and thinking about how the information presented by the family may be viewed *differently* from the way in which the family currently view the issues, and from a new perspective.

Within this way of working, where the family listen directly to the team's ideas, it is obviously important that the reflecting team do not convey information in a way which could be construed by the family as negative. This, in itself, can be important in helping to develop an open and respectful approach when discussing issues which families present to us. Anderson also suggests that the nature of the ideas we present can be very important for change in the family system. He suggests that, if the ideas reflected to the family and therapist are either too 'unusual' or 'not unusual enough', they will have little impact upon the family system. If the ideas are too unusual, the family may not be able to accept them, and if the ideas are too like the family's own ideas, the family may accept them but there will be no change in the family system, and it will be a system which stands still. The objective of the team is to introduce perspectives which can be accepted by the family system, but which are sufficiently different to facilitate change.

Power and Hierarchies in the Team

Working as a reflecting team may have a number of advantages for the balance of communication and hierarchies within the team. Many multidisciplinary teams working with older adults are made up of a range of professionals, who will each have a particular role and position within the team. This role may change depending upon the task in hand, and in different contexts. There are various settings in which professional hierarchies and power are important, and it may be necessary for effective resource management and decision making to have an effective team hierarchy and clearly defined professional roles in some circumstances. One example of this may be when decisions are made about the use of inpatient hospital beds, where someone with an overall perspective on the service may be needed to make decisions about use of this resource. Different professionals may also have clearly defined roles in an in-patient setting which are somewhat different from one another. However, when working therapeutically with families as a team, professional hierarchies may be less relevant, but they may nevertheless continue to have an impact upon team working.

Reflecting Ideas Sequentially

Adopting a reflecting team approach may help to diffuse hierarchical positions within the team when working with families, as *all* team members have an opportunity to contribute a view. This is particularly the case if the team reflect their views *sequentially*, that is, if each person takes a turn to contribute a different perspective concerning the family interview. This may be to contribute a new idea or to build on the contribution or ideas of someone else in the team, without interruption from other team members. Thus each team member may contribute a view in a particular sequence, and the process may continue until they feel that they are not able to contribute any new information and/or that contributions are becoming repetitive.

Using this reflecting team approach, the family are able to listen to contributions of all of the team, without the most strongly voiced position being the *only* perspective presented to the family. Lynn Hoffman (1990) notes that within group settings, the more vocal members of the group (the 'lions'), often dominate the proceedings, whereas quieter group members, or perhaps those in a lower position in the prevailing team hierarchy (the 'lambs'), may be silent. Many families may benefit from hearing the ideas of the 'lambs', but some methods of team working in services for older adults do not allow this to occur effectively. Many teams who work together frequently may benefit from the reflecting team approach as it interrupts the established communication pattern of the team, which may have become repetitive and lacking in creativity over the years, and which may reflect hierarchies in the system of the team, rather than enhancing opportunities for important contributions to be made by *all* members of the team.

Services for older people and their families often utilise a team-working approach, and there are many different ways in which ideas concerning reflecting teams may be applied to team-working with older people.

Working with Families in the Home Environment

A way of working with families supported by colleagues has been described by Smith and Kingston (1980), this method can readily be used in the home environment. In their *live supervision* model one clinician interviews the family while a colleague sits in the same room, listening. The colleague may intervene from time to time to speak to the clinician to reflect ideas or to ask the clinician whether they wish to address a particular issue with the family. If two or more colleagues are able to be present it would be possible for them to work as a reflecting team, presenting ideas and different perspectives to the clinician and the family. They would be able to do this directly while sitting in the same room, without the need for the special resources or technology required to utilise the reverse sound and vision system described above. This method would be suitable for use in the homes of clients and their families, which is often the environmental focus for work in services for elderly people.

Co-Therapists Working with Families

An alternative model would be for two clinicians to work as co-therapists, but to do so in such a way that they function as a 'smaller scale' reflecting team. In this example, both clinicians may interview and talk with the family, but they may take different roles, in that one clinician 'speaks more' and the other clinician 'listens more'. The clinician whose role is primarily to be an active listener may also be able to contribute reflections on the process of the interview and the issues being discussed, which may help to introduce new ideas to the family system.

There are a number of ways in which this co-therapy approach can be helpful when working with older people. If the older person in the family has a disability which makes it difficult for them to contribute equally to the discussion, for example, a sensory impairment or a dementing illness, the 'listening' clinician may seek from the outset to be the older person's advocate and to ensure that they have the opportunity to contribute to the session. They may, for example, reflect to the co-worker and family that they have not heard the older person speak for some time and ask for space to allow this to occur. Alternatively the clinician may seek to *reframe* or reword a point to help the older person to participate.

If the older person is unable to contribute verbally, the 'listening' clinician may ask other members of the family to reflect upon what they feel the older person would like to contribute if they were able to do so, or to ask who in the family most feels they can reflect the older person's perspective on the issues being discussed (Circular Questions).

Other ways in which working with a co-worker when seeing older people and their families can be helpful include situations where the elderly person and their family have both psychological needs and needs for practical solutions and support. Two team workers with differing areas of expertise and professional background may be able to 'work together', and to address both of these needs effectively within a meeting with the family. Co-working in this situation may also help prevent artificial distinctions from being made between helpful practical ideas and helpful ideas which provide psychological support, as it is likely that many older people and their families may benefit from both forms of help, and that the two forms of help will tend to complement one another. Practical solutions often help provide psychological benefits as they reduce levels of stress, and psychological support often helps the client to view practical solutions in a different way. Co-workers can split responsibilities in other ways within a family meeting, for example, one therapist may concentrate on verbal communication in the family, while the other concentrates particularly on non-verbal communication.

Co-workers are also able to enter into a dialogue within the session, and this technique may be used to help the family system. The co-workers may 'model' calm dialogue by reflecting with one another about issues in the family in a relaxed manner, and this may be helpful when working with a family whose communication style appears to prevent listening calmly to one another. Alternatively, co-workers may 'model' the possibility of 'disagreeing' or having alternate points of view by reflecting upon *different* ideas in front of a family who are stuck with repeating the same patterns and cannot communicate different viewpoints to one another. Working with a colleague can also help to provide important emotional support for clinicians who may be working with a large family system facing many complex and difficult issues.

John Carpenter (1993) has addressed a number of issues associated with co-working which are involved when two clinicians prepare to work together productively.

Case Reviews and Case Conferences

When working with older adults, multiple agencies are often involved in care delivery and in the assessment process, and case review meetings or case conferences are therefore often a useful way to bring together professional staff, the client and their family, and to provide an important opportunity to share information. Ideas about reflecting teams may be applied and utilised in a case review or case conference. One possible model for this is as follows.

1   The case conference takes place with the client, keyworker and members of the professional team present. In many cases it may

be appropriate and important to seek the client's permission to invite family members too.

2   The keyworker helps the client and family to present information about the current situation and important issues from *their own perspective*. The keyworker may have to take a less or more active role, depending upon the client(s) and their capacity to verbalise the main issues, but should nevertheless try to present the issues from the client's perspective.

3   The rest of the team may then reflect upon these issues in front of the client and keyworker. They may raise issues from their own professional perspectives, which they feel are important to the client's assessment or care.

4   The client, family and keyworker discuss, *together* with the team, any changes to the care plan, and the keyworker produces a written summary of the care plan which is circulated to all those present, including the client and family.

This model for running a case review or conference may not differ substantially from many other reviews at which the client is present. However the above model particularly emphasises the need to listen to the client's own perspective *first*, and the need for the keyworker to assist the client in presenting their views. The client and keyworker then benefit from hearing the views of the different members of the team, who direct their communication, and present their perspectives in a way which is as meaningful as possible, *to the client and keyworker* rather than to a designated leader or consultant in the team. The review thus remains client-focused and the care plan is more likely to be formulated in a way which is meaningful for the client and in a way which the client can understand.

Team Case Discussions

While the above model allows the team to reflect views about care with the client present, it is also possible to use ideas about reflecting teams to help team members generate ideas about clients who they feel 'stuck' with or unable to progress with, and where the client is not present. Here the team member, who will often be the client's keyworker, presents the difficulties they are having with a particular case, and the team reflect upon the issues facing their colleague and try to help the keyworker to progress with the situation. The 'case' in this situation may either be an individual client or a client and their family. One example of a team case discussion follows.

1   The keyworker or team member presents a brief summary of the case and the difficulties the keyworker is having making progress.
2   The team sit in a circle and reflect in sequence about the situation. Each team member tries either to build upon previous ideas or to introduce a new perspective. It is important that the team sit in a circle as this often helps the flow of communication, and helps prevent individual members feeling excluded from the team.
3   Team members can 'pass' if they can think of no contribution, but should try to contribute something, remembering Anderson's opinion that unusual views can often help to shift perspectives on a case, and that it is therefore important to remember that all ideas do not *have* to conform to those which the team would usually expect to hear. There are no 'wrong' or 'right' ideas, but there are different ideas, any of which may be helpful in different circumstances.
4   Team members wait for their turn to speak and should not interrupt the circle of ideas by commenting on what colleagues are saying or interrupting with ideas 'out of turn'. This ensures that all team members have an equal opportunity to contribute their ideas.
5   The keyworker sits outside the circle and may note down ideas which the team's discussion produces. The keyworker does not comment upon the ideas (for example, to say 'I've already tried that' or 'The family don't want that to happen'), but can ask the team to reflect further upon a particular issue relevant to the case which they feel may be helpful.
6   The team continue to reflect ideas until the keyworker feels they are no longer generating new perspectives; for example, the team may be 'passing' frequently or repeating the same ideas more than once.
7   Reflections conclude with the keyworker describing which ideas they feel will help them working with the client(s) and identifying

one or two which they will seek to develop further or to explore with the case.

Teaching Sessions and Workshops

The steps which are described above for team case discussions can also be usefully employed in teaching sessions and workshops. Here the leader of the session may ask the participants to reflect as a group or in small groups about particular issues or case examples. This can often be an effective way of generating a wide range of ideas, and also of encouraging everyone present to participate and contribute to the session.

CHAPTER 7

FAMILIES:
Examining our own position

THIS CHAPTER CONSIDERS how it can be important to reflect upon our own beliefs and values when working with families. It considers how we may have acquired a number of beliefs from our family of origin, which have an impact upon our work with later-life families, and introduces an exercise which explores this further.

Different models of therapy, including family therapy, involve the therapist disclosing aspects of themselves to clients to different degrees. Traditionally some of the early systemic models of family therapy involved the therapist adopting a position of 'neutrality' (Palazzoli-Selvini *et al*, 1980), where subjectivity on the part of the therapist was discouraged. Within these early models the therapist often tried to maintain some emotional distance from the family, and thus to remain 'outside' the family system, in an attempt to adopt an objective position. The tools and equipment sometimes used by family therapists, such as video cameras and one-way screens, were seen by some to reinforce the position of the therapist as a distant expert using complicated techniques. However, more recently, increased attention has been given to the way families feel about the process of family therapy, and to the ways in which the role of the therapist affects the family's experience. Carpenter and Treacher (1993), for example, have written about the importance of 'user-friendly' family therapy, where a task of the therapist is to: 'build working alliances with families so that they feel empowered to help themselves' (p4).

This represents a shift away from the position of the therapist as a somewhat distant expert to a more collaborative approach, where the therapist tries to work in partnership with the family. However, avoiding the stance of 'powerful expert' does not mean that the therapist should not be seen to have skills which can be brought to the session and which the family can value. The engaging skills of the therapist, taking account of the family's cultural and social system, become very important if the therapist is to be able to work collaboratively and successfully with the family in this way. The ability to develop a rapport with the family and put family members at ease, and to introduce questions and ideas which help them to perceive their situation in a different way, is also important.

There are many factors which may influence our ability to establish an effective working relationship with families. Some of these factors relate to characteristics of the environment and the other professionals with whom we are working, some relate to the characteristics of families and the individuals within them, and some relate to ourselves. Some of the obstacles to effective working with families can arise from our own beliefs and perceptions of families with whom we are working. Our beliefs can be powerfully positive in helping us to generate ideas and hypotheses which guide our work, but our beliefs can also be restricting, particularly if we do not recognise and challenge the ways in which they may affect our work. There are many ways in which our beliefs about older adults and families may affect our working practice. Some of our beliefs may originate from general views and attitudes held by society and the culture within which we operate, about ageing and the late life cycle. Within Western society we often tend to hold a number of negative and often stereotypical beliefs about the ageing process, which may influence our own beliefs and adversely affect the range of opportunities for therapy which we offer to older people within health care services.

We are also likely to be affected and influenced, at another level, by the beliefs held within our own families about the position of older people in the family and relationships with older people. Being aware of the messages and ideas which come from our own family of origin and which govern the ways in which we relate to members of our own families can help us to progress in our work with families and in our professional lives. An increased awareness may be achieved in many different ways, and may include exercises described earlier in this book, such as reviewing our own genograms and family maps and considering relationships within our own families in pictorial form. One exercise used frequently by the team I work with, which is routinely introduced when a new member of staff joins, is for each team member to briefly present their own genogram, drawing out the issues which seem most important to them at that point in time. At intervals we re-present our genograms, outlining any important changes or new themes which are important to our own family systems. We find this helps to raise an awareness within ourselves of important themes and issues within our families, and also helps other team members to understand issues which may have an impact upon our work. This enables team members to help one another to explore this further at a later point should, for example, similar themes and issues emerge in the families with whom a particular team member is working, and when it appears to be affecting their work.

There are many general themes which it can also be helpful for us to address with respect to the beliefs of ourselves and our own families of origin in relation to the later life stages of the life cycle. We may hypothesise about some of the important late life cycle events which were introduced in Chapter 5, and consider how our own beliefs about late life cycle events may be important to our personal and professional lives. Common themes may be who cares for frailer older people in our families or what the beliefs of our family of origin are about community versus institutional care; or we may consider which illnesses had an impact upon the lives or caused the death of members of our families. We may also reflect upon the positive effects of ageing and our own families' perceptions of the developmental opportunities which the ageing process affords.

Another way of considering the impact of our family of origin upon our beliefs and our work with older people and their families is to try the exercise suggested below. I am indebted to colleagues from the Prudence Skynner Family Therapy Team for Older Adults, for allowing me to include this exercise.

Examining our Views about Ageing

1   Think about the messages you received when growing up within your family about growing old and being old. Write down five or six key/important messages which you acquired for either gender relating to some of the following topics: intimacy, bodies, showing emotions, race, sex, family life, culture, chores, facing change, death, living arrangements, caring for others, gender, class, death, social activities, work and retirement, physical health.

2   Share your list with that of a colleague or team member.
    How are the lists the same and different ?
    Which messages do you still have some use for ?
    In what way may these messages affect the way you work?

When deciding whether to adopt an individual therapeutic approach or a family/systems approach, there are numerous factors which will influence the decision. At the most basic level, family and systems work concentrates upon systems of relationships between individuals as the main focus for change, rather than focusing change at the level of the *individual* older person per se. If we work with the older person as an individual in therapy, we are working with their account of their own reality and we may not necessarily seek their understanding of their family and the family system within which they operate. If we meet the older person *and* their family, we introduce many different dimensions, as we may directly seek the perspective of other family members too. We may also seek their views about their part in the family system and about the parts played by others within it, including the older person. Some of the decision about the type of approach to adopt may be determined by the clinician, but the perspective and views of the older adult and their family is important too.

In some ways it could be said that, if families seek help from outside agencies, it may be indicative of a sense of disempowerment within the family. It may even be seen to be indicative of a decline in the power of ageing family members, who in many cultures are traditionally seen to hold wisdom and power which allows them to help younger family members to negotiate and resolve the challenges of earlier stages of the life cycle within the family. Older family members, as a consequence of increasing social change and geographical mobility within families, may have lost many of the direct functions associated with advice and wisdom giver in the extended family system. On the other hand, seeking professional help with respect to family issues may be viewed positively as an example of families who face later life issues making a choice to draw upon other resources. The therapist's position here will be important, and the therapist can encourage family empowerment by adopting a stance which acknowledges the resources of the therapist but also acknowledges the many resources of the family, including its older family members, too.

Fundamentally, within our family therapy clinic we are trying to offer families an experience which is of some value to the older person and also to other family members, and are trying to work together with families to enable change to occur. However, different people may value the same experience in different ways. Each family member may take away a different perspective from a family interview, which may help them in different ways. In our family clinic, we have experienced families where, within the same family, some members attribute any change to the therapists, others attribute it to their own efforts in therapy, and others again believe no change has occurred at all. Bloch (1993) debates what is of value in family therapy:

> ... something of value must be exchanged. What is that? One can minimize power, sanitize it, share it; one can acknowledge its complexities and vagaries, for example, that there are ways that clients hold therapists in thrall. The exchanges are multilayered. But, something of value must be exchanged. What is that? (pxiv)

Here we have *the* question. We can offer our time and exchanges of words, but determining what is valuable in family therapy is a question which, perhaps, only the families we see can fully answer. We should explore this question more often with the families we meet.

CHAPTER 8

CLOSING CASES

THE FOLLOWING CASE EXAMPLES illustrate some of the cases referred to the Central Manchester family team and invite you to reflect upon some of the ideas introduced earlier in the book. Administrative materials used by the family team are provided subsequently for your information.

The case examples invite you to try out some of the techniques and ideas introduced in this book, in particular the use of genograms, hypothesising and circular questions, as well as reflecting a little upon the life cycle issues which may be important to the family concerned. In each case a brief family scenario is presented, based upon actual examples of clinical work.

It is important to acknowledge, as discussed earlier in the book, that there is unlikely to be a single hypothesis or intervention plan which will 'solve' the difficulties which family members present, and that it is not usually productive to believe that some interventions will be *right* and others *wrong*, because different ideas may affect different family members in different ways. It is more likely that there will be a range of ideas, reflections and interventions which the therapist can share with the family in order to enable family members to progress. Remembering the ideas discussed in Chapter 6 may be helpful. At the stage of generating ideas and hypotheses about the family system it can often be helpful to 'brainstorm' and to try to generate ideas which may initially seem 'unusual', as well as generating ideas which are more 'usual' or seemingly 'commonplace'. This can be a creative and freeing process, enabling a wide range of possibilities to be considered.

However not all of these ideas will be explored with the family and it may be worth recalling Tom Anderson's suggestion that ideas, shared with the family, which are 'too unusual' may be difficult for the family to identify with, and may therefore not enable change to occur. On the other hand, ideas which are 'too usual' may also fail to promote change as they may too closely resemble the ideas which the family have already tried for themselves and, if they had had a successful impact, the family would not be attending the family therapy session.

Referrals to the Family Team

The following are examples of referrals seen by the family team. A selection from these referrals is considered in further detail below, but this brief résumé of a range of referrals demonstrates the wide range of presenting difficulties which may be addressed using a family/systems approach to work with older adults and their families.

Case 1

Mr D is a frail 69-year-old man, who has suffered a severe stroke and has a dense left hemiplegia. His mood has been very labile, and he is currently living in a nursing home. His family had complained about the standard of care he received in a previous nursing home, leading to his moving to the present one. However the family are still unhappy with the standard of care, and there have been disagreements in the family about whether he should remain there or return to live with his wife at home. His wife visits the nursing home frequently and he has nine surviving children, who contribute to a rota of visiting him at the nursing home. There have been many disagreements in the family about the rota, and there was marked conflict about it at the time of referral. Some of the children are angry that they contribute more time to visiting their father than do other family members. Some of the family members have asked social services to move him to another home, and social services have referred the family to the family team for help.

Case 2

Mrs A is an inpatient on a psychiatric ward and has been receiving treatment for depression. She moved to the UK from Pakistan in 1953 and is now 65 years old. She lives with her husband. Her daughter lives nearby and works full time, is married and has three children. She visits her parents frequently and has a close relationship with them. Mrs A's son is married, has no children and lives in America. It had always been expected that Mrs A and her husband would move to live with their son in America when Mr A retired, and the son has recently arranged to have an extension built on his house in order to enable them to move there. Mrs A's daughter has expressed the view to ward nurses that her mother has never wanted to move to America, as she has friends in her local community and would miss the contact with her daughter and grandchildren if she moved. Mr A strongly believes that they should move to live with their son, but does not wish to persuade his wife to do so while she remains unwell and depressed. Mrs A's daughter feels that her mother cannot tell Mr A about her reservations about moving to America. Mrs A's depression has not responded to treatment while she has been in hospital and the psychiatrist has referred the family to the family team.

Case 3

Mrs G is 74 and has a long history of anxiety; she has recently complained of some forgetfulness. She was recently referred by her family doctor to mental health services for help following the death of her grandson, James, aged 14, during an epileptic seizure at home, which was precipitated by the flicker from the television screen. Mrs G lives with her daughter, son in law and grandchildren. Since the death of James, Mrs G's daughter has been drinking heavily, and James' 11 year old brother has been attending school sporadically. James had also attended school sporadically prior to his death and, at the time of his death, Mrs G had let him stay in the house rather than attend school. His mother and father did not approve of this. All of the family are extremely distressed about James' death and the circumstances of it. The doctor has asked the family team to see the family.

Case 4

Mrs P is a 66-year-old woman who has recently presented to psychiatric services with severe depression. She had attempted suicide. Her husband has recently retired and a woman with whom he had recently ended a twenty-year affair has been phoning their home repeatedly. Mr P had carried on the affair with this work colleague without Mrs P's knowledge, but had decided to end it and to try to be loyal to his wife following his retirement. The phone calls began when he ended the relationship and Mrs P therefore found out about the affair. Mr and Mrs P have two children, one of whom believes his mother should try to accept his father's apology and try to 'move on' and develop her relationship with him. The other son feels very angry with his father and feels his mother's response has been completely understandable. Mrs P is currently in hospital and is trying to decide whether or not to remain in the relationship with her husband.

Case 5

Mr B had begun to consult his family doctor very frequently, complaining of many physical health problems. He reports head and stomach pain, dizziness and has had a number of 'fainting attacks'. Prior to this he rarely visited the doctor and despite rigorous investigation no explanation for the physical symptoms has been found. Mr B lives with his daughter, Ann, aged 42, who has recently begun a relationship with John. This is Ann's first serious relationship and she had been considering moving in with John. However, she has confided to the doctor that she does not feel she can do so while her father appears to be so ill, and she had visited the doctor asking for a sick note as she has herself felt depressed and unable to go to work, as she has worried about who will look after her father while she is out of the house. The doctor has referred them to the family team.

Case 6

Mrs D has recently consulted her family doctor. She is 83 and has been experiencing heart problems and increasing pain from arthritis over the past two years. In addition her husband's health is failing and she has been trying to care for him. For many years she has also felt responsible for the care of her younger stepsister, Joan, who is 70, has a long history of mental health problems and also has mild learning disabilities. Joan's daughter, Susan, has long-standing problems with alcohol and drug abuse, and Joan often gives her money from her pension to buy drugs and food. Susan has threatened Joan physically when she has refused to give her money. Mrs D feels she has been able to support Joan effectively over the years in refusing Susan's demands and with respect to Joan's mental health problems, but is finding this an increasing burden with her own failing health. She has asked the doctor for help and he has advised her to contact social services and to seek support from the family team.

Case 7

Mr F is a 79-year-old man with Alzheimer's disease. He has moderate cognitive impairment and lives with his wife and son, in a house which he signed over to his son five years ago. Their son plans to marry soon and to move his partner into the house. The son has contacted social services, reporting that he can no longer cope with his father and would like him to move into residential care. Mr F is strongly opposed to this idea and wants to remain with his wife at the family home. Social services have substantially increased the support services given to him at home, and he attends a day centre three times a week. His wife wants him to remain at home with her. On one occasion the son took him to the accident and emergency department at the local hospital and left him there, saying he could no longer live at the house, but Mr F got into a taxi and returned home. The family team have been asked to see the family.

Case 8

Mrs S (Diane) is a 67-year-old woman who has been presenting frequently to her family doctor for some months reporting anxiety symptoms. The doctor could not identify any precipitant for the symptoms but felt they were quite mild and had not recommended any treatment. However the doctor had felt concerned because Mrs S had described how she felt her anxiety symptoms were particularly affecting her daughter. Mrs S felt that her daughter, Jane, had recently begun to complain of similar anxiety symptoms and that these had become so severe that Jane was no longer able to leave the house unaccompanied. Jane was also crying frequently. Mother and daughter had begun to do everything together, and felt unable to do anything, such as speaking to neighbours, shopping, or attending the doctor's clinic, without the other person being present. They had also reduced contact with other family members. The doctor referred them to the family clinic for an opinion.

Some of the above cases will now be explored in further detail and some of the approaches and ideas introduced earlier in this text will be considered with respect to them.

CASE 8 Mrs S (Diane) and Jane

With respect to this case, there are a number of questions which can be generated from the brief referral information, and which it may be useful to reflect upon.

Why is Diane presenting with anxiety symptoms now?
Why are they having the effects described upon Jane, her daughter?

What are the effects of Diane and Jane doing everything together? What function may this be serving? What would happen if they did things separately?

Why has contact with other family members reduced?

In this case Diane and Jane were seen for an initial appointment. They discussed the feelings of anxiety they were both experiencing, and the ways in which this limited their lives. Further information was gathered about the family and you may wish to use the information below to draw a genogram of the family including as much information as possible about ages, names, relationships and births. In this genogram it would be interesting to pay particular attention to recurrent patterns across generations of the family (transgenerational issues).

Diane is 67 years old and has four children, each of whom has a different father. Both of her parents, Bill and Suzie, are dead. She did not wish to give the names of any of her partners when the information about her family was collected as she said none of them had remained in contact with her or the children after the relationships ended. Her eldest son, David, now 52, was born when Diane was still living at home with her parents, and she described how she had kept the pregnancy secret until she was seven months pregnant. Following the birth her father refused to let her continue to live in their house, and Diane went to live with an aunt. David was subsequently adopted and Diane has no contact with him. She again became pregnant two years later and had a son called Frederick, who was also adopted by another couple. Diane has limited contact with him by letter and he now lives overseas. Diane worked in paid employment during her twenties and moved into a flat. When she was 28 she became pregnant and married a man whom she described as 'violent' and 'a heavy drinker'. She had a daughter, Joanne, from this marriage, and although the marriage lasted for ten years, she described this as an unhappy time, and the marriage ended in divorce. She subsequently had a brief relationship with a man when she was 43 and Jane was born. The man lived briefly with Diane, Joanne and Jane and then left. Diane heard that he had died about five years previously. Jane has always lived with Diane, and Jane has never had personal relationships. They remain in close contact with Joanne (39), who has one son, aged 24, from a childhood pregnancy, and a daughter aged 15 from a marriage which ended in divorce. There is no contact between Joanne's children and their fathers. Joanne has recently commenced a relationship with a man whom both Jane and Diane say they 'do not like'.

Genogram
The genogram may look as represented below:

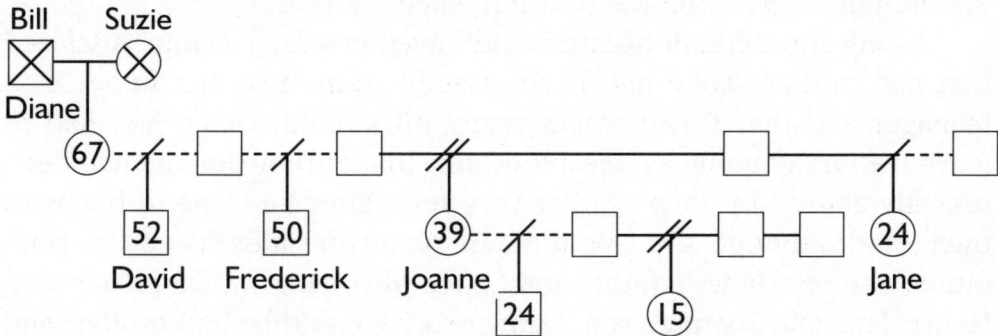

Have you identified any of the recurring themes in this family?

- Diane had a childhood pregnancy at the age of 15, which produced a son, David. Her daughter, Joanne, also became pregnant at 15 and had a son. Joanne's daughter is now 15.
- Joanne had her son at about the same time as Diane had Jane.
- Diane and Joanne have both given birth to more than one child who have different fathers.
- Fathers in the family do not often remain in contact with their children.
- Family members who remain in close contact are female.
- Both Diane and Jane are reporting anxiety symptoms.

In a subsequent family appointment, Diane and Jane invited Joanne along too. A genogram was drawn with them and there was some discussion about who felt most close to whom in the family. Joanne was angry about her mother and sister's views about her new partner and described how she felt Diane and Jane had 'been rude' to him when they were introduced. Jane expressed the view that Joanne's new partner made her feel very anxious, and felt that Joanne had been spending much less time with her and her mother since meeting him. Joanne felt this was because her sister and mother did not want her to visit if her partner was with her and Joanne described how her new partner was bringing lots of positive experiences into her life. Diane expressed the view that 'Joanne and her daughter [Rosie] would only be made unhappy' as a result of Joanne's new relationship. Joanne became very angry at this point and replied that her mother and sister 'should not keep letting the past influence the present'.

A long and difficult discussion followed in which Joanne disclosed that her mother Diane had been sexually abused by her father as a teenager and that David was actually Bill's child. Diane had had to leave the family home as a result of this. In addition, Joanne had been sexually abused by Jane's father very soon after he came to live with them, and although she was not sure about the identity of her son's father, she felt Janes's father may have also been father to her son. Hence Jane and Joanne's son, both aged 24, could be half-brother and sister as well as aunt and nephew.

Diane and Jane were initially angry that Joanne had disclosed this information in the session, but made no attempt to prevent her doing so and replied that they felt 'Joanne should keep telling' when the therapists checked with them whether they were comfortable for the therapists to continue to listen to Joanne's account. They agreed they would attend for a further appointment.

They subsequently did attend the next appointment, without Joanne, and were able to begin to talk about the impact of these events upon their lives. Jane talked about how she had not been sexually abused herself but had been aware of the abuse of her mother and sister, and felt this had 'put her off men'. Diane expressed regret that she had not been able to establish a happy and lasting relationship with a man during her life and expressed guilt because she felt that this had affected Jane's chances of having happy relationships too. She did not feel that either herself or Jane would be likely to have happy relationships with men in the future, and that they were 'better keeping each other company'. Over subsequent sessions they were able to explore the ways in which these beliefs and experiences were affecting their current relationship with one another, and discussed how they had felt a need to 'stick together' and support one another, but that this had resulted in their sharing negative experiences with anxiety too.

We were able to reflect further on the genogram and to discuss why the anxiety had come to the fore at that point. One hypothesis which was explored in relation to 'why now?' was to do with Joanne's new relationship. We noted that Joanne's daughter, at the age of 15, may have been perceived as 'vulnerable' in the family, as she was reaching an age at which both Diane and Joanne had experienced sexual abuse and pregnancy in the past, and wondered whether they were afraid that Joanne's new partner might be a 'risk' to her. Diane had experienced these fears but Jane said she had not. Jane perceived the new relationship as threatening in terms of a man establishing contact with the family which she would have preferred not to have, rather than directly as a threat to Joanne's daughter. They had preferred trying to avoid contact with Joanne as it also meant having contact with her new male partner.

These reflections helped in our understanding of the questions, based on the brief referral information, which we raised at the beginning of work with this case (see above).

Over subsequent sessions, some of which were attended by Joanne, it was possible to discuss and negotiate how Jane and Diane could have 'safe' or comfortable contact with Joanne's new partner, and over the months their fears about him 'as a risk' reduced. They were also able to negotiate how they might begin to establish contact with more people outside their close family relationship, and both Jane and Diane were able to go out socially with friends whom they had previously seen more of. Diane felt that her anxiety levels subsided to a point where she was able to go out independently of Jane, and Jane's anxiety levels reduced more rapidly due to this. Some time was also spent reflecting upon the genogram, and talking about the way recurring patterns across generations of the family, and recurring events at the same stage of various family members' life cycles, had created an expectation that recurring patterns would continue to occur, particularly if they were negative experiences.

This was an example of a situation where the presenting problem of anxiety was in the setting of considerable pressures which had a family context. The use of the genogram, and discussion of recurring themes in the family which arose from this, led to difficult discussions initiated by a family member, Joanne, who had not herself sought help initially. Disclosures about sensitive issues such as sexual abuse obviously need to be handled carefully in a therapy session, and the therapists took care to check that Jane and Diane wished to have Joanne continue to speak after she made the initial disclosures. Diane and Jane both took the view that they were initially angry with Joanne, but that they also felt a sense of relief that she had shared their dilemmas with us. They did not feel they had been able to discuss these issues with one another because of a fear of upsetting one another, but that meeting in the family clinic had enabled them to do this. There have been many discussions of the legacy of childhood sexual abuse for people presenting to mental health services in adulthood, and this was an example of the way in which sexual abuse had impacted upon different generations of a family and across older and younger family members.

CASE 2 Mrs A

From the brief referral information above, concerning Mrs A, a number of questions may be identified:

Why has Mrs A become depressed now? (Why now?)

What function may the depression be serving? What would happen if Mrs A was not depressed?

What are Mrs A's/the family's views of her admission to a psychiatric ward and their beliefs about her low mood within the family's cultural context?

How can the family therapists try to develop an understanding of how the family's ethnicity and cultural background may be important to the family's views and decisions about where Mr and Mrs A choose to live?

What would the impact be on different family members if Mr A and Mrs A chose (a) to stay in the UK or (b) to move to the United States to live with their son? Who would be most affected in the family? How would they be affected?

The family were referred by the psychiatrist. What is the psychiatrist's understanding concerning why Mrs A's depression has not responded to treatment? Has this understanding been communicated to the family?

In this case Mrs A, Mr A, the son, daughter in law and daughter attended a family session. The son and his wife were visiting from the United States. Mrs A was still a hospital inpatient. Discussion centred around Mrs A's understanding of her low mood and the family's understanding of this. Mrs A felt that she would not 'get better', whereas Mr A and the son were optimistic that her mood would improve and that this would enable her to sell the house in the UK and move to America. The daughter did not feel able to express a view about her mother's mood but believed that her mother did not wish to move to America.

The family shared with the family therapists their cultural perspective that, traditionally, the eldest son of the family would provide for his parents in later life. The son had taken this responsibility seriously and had built an extension onto his house in the United States in order to enable his parents to move to live with himself and his wife. He and his wife had no children and expressed a desire to care for their parents in later life. The daughter-in-law felt that as she did not work outside of the home, she would be able to cook meals and care for Mr and Mrs A and that they could therefore 'take it easy' in their retirement.

The daughter described how her parents had worked hard to develop links and friendships in their community when they moved to the UK in 1953, and now had a number of supportive long-standing friendships. The daughter visited them daily and her children were in close contact with them too. She was concerned that her parents would find it hard to develop similar supports in the United States and felt that her brother had fewer contacts with the Pakistani community there than was the case for her parents in the UK. She was concerned that her parents would feel isolated and might lose their independence.

Hypotheses

On the basis of the information gathered so far, it is possible to generate a number of ideas and hypotheses about the family system:

- If Mrs A 'becomes well' her husband, son and daughter in law would want her to move to America.
- The cultural perspective of the family is important to their beliefs about how and where Mrs A may spend a happy late life.
- Different family members, at different stages of the life cycle, have different views about what may be helpful.
- A move to America may reduce the social supports which Mr and Mrs A have established in the UK and will reduce contact with the daughter and grandchildren. This may increase Mrs A's vulnerability to depression.
- The son and daughter-in-law may see caring for Mr and Mrs A as a positive family role for them. They do not have children and the daughter-in-law feels it would be a positive role for her to care for Mr and Mrs A. Being a carer, who is 'needed', may fulfil important emotional needs for the daughter-in-law. However this may conflict with Mrs (and Mr?) A's expectations for their retirement, and possible expectations of a more independent later life.

Further discussion with the family centred around some of the differences in perspective between different family members. The two (white) therapists shared with the family their desire to try to develop an understanding of how cultural perspectives were important to the family's decision making and offered to provide a forum in which the family could try to come to some consensus about the future, and to consider whether compromise was possible.

The daughter immediately and clearly wished to discuss the question of compromise more fully. She felt that the decision for her parents to move to America had been an expectation which the family had had for many years, and that it was a decision which was grounded in family tradition and which the family had never questioned or considered compromising upon. She felt that, if her parents sold their house in the UK, there would be little possibility of compromise and that they would find it hard to spend much time in the UK in the future. She felt her mother was attached to her home and should not sell it, but should instead spend some time in the UK and some time in America. Mrs A agreed that she had found the prospect of selling her home very distressing and that this worry was a factor contributing to her low mood. She had assumed the house would be sold because this had been the assumption of the family for many years, even though the house did not need to be sold for financial reasons.

This generated considerable discussion between the family members, and the family were able to explore a number of options and compromises; some of which they viewed as more or less desirable. The family were able to agree that Mrs A's mood was unlikely to improve while she was faced with the prospect of selling her home and moving to America. They were able to negotiate a compromise whereby Mr and Mrs A would visit the son for periods of time in America but would retain their home base in the UK near their daughter too.

Throughout this process the therapists attempted to adopt a role of facilitator to the discussion and tried to avoid directing the family's decision-making process in any particular direction. Working with families in which there are age differences and also cultural differences between therapists and referred clients can be a difficult task, but also a very rewarding experience. The situation is likely to generate very different perspectives as to what may be the 'right solution' and it is important that the therapists' 'right solution' is not imposed on the family. The task for the therapists here was to offer the family a forum for discussion at a place away from the home and the therapists helped the family to generate their own solutions and pathways to change.

Circular questions are a particularly useful device when attempting to fulfil this role as a therapist as they invite the family to reflect upon different perspectives which different family members have on the situation. As Street and Dryden (1988) wrote, effective circular questions should leave the family reflecting on their answers to the questions and upon the issues the questions have raised for them, rather than upon the detail of the questions asked. Circular questions were used extensively by the therapists with this family, and some examples of the questions asked follow.

Q: What do different family members do when Mrs A describes feeling depressed? (Sequential circular question.)

A: Mr A had tried to persuade her that she would feel happier if she moved to live in America. The daughter visits her more often to offer support.

Q: Who in the family would be most affected if Mr and Mrs A moved to America? Who most/least tries to persuade Mrs A that moving to America is a good idea? Who, in the family, is most/least affected by Mrs A's low mood? (Classification circular question.)

A: The family felt Mrs A and her daughter would be most affected if she moved to America. They felt that Mr A and her son most tried to persuade her to move. They felt that Mr A was most affected by Mrs A's low mood.

Q: How did the family think the relationship between Mr and Mrs A had been different since Mrs A became depressed? How did the family think the relationship between Mrs A and other family members had changed since she became depressed? (Diachronic circular questions.)

A: Mr A had initially responded to Mrs A's depression by trying to persuade her to move to America, in the hope that this would help her mood. Her daughter had developed a closer relationship and more contact with her. The son was visiting more often from America as he felt concerned about her.

Q: If Mrs A's depression did not lift, what did the family think would happen? (Hypothetical circular question.)

A: The family agreed that they did not think Mrs A could move to America whilst her mood remained as depressed as it was at present.

Case 1: Mr D

Mr D (Donald) and his family were referred to the family team by the social services department. Donald had been the main carer for his 63-year-old wife, Beryl, who had a long history of chronic chest problems and arthritis. Her health problems restricted her mobility considerably. Donald had undertaken most household tasks, cooking, cleaning and caring for Beryl, and had often declined offers of assistance from his children, telling them that they had their own lives to lead. Unfortunately Donald had suffered a severe stroke, nine months before, which had left him with a dense left hemiplegia. His mood at the time of referral was labile, and his cognitive function, in particular his memory abilities, and visuospatial functioning were markedly impaired. He was unable to attend to activities of daily living without physical assistance and his mobility was very poor. Following a period in hospital, he had been discharged to a nursing home, where he remained for six weeks. His family made several complaints about the standard of care in the nursing home and he was moved by social services to the nursing home where he was residing at the time of referral to the family team. Social services were financing his care, and were also providing assistance with carers at home for Beryl.

Donald and Beryl had 11 children. The following information may be used as the basis for a genogram. Donald (69) and Beryl (63) have six surviving daughters and three sons, and most continue to visit Donald and Beryl on a regular basis. They range in age from 20 to 43. Joan, the eldest daughter, is married and has two daughters, both of whom have two young children. Margaret is 42 and married, with three sons and one grandchild, followed closely by her brother, Edward, who is 41 and married, with no children. Philip has never married and is 39. His twin brother was stillborn. Amanda is 33, unmarried and living in Australia. Simon is 32 and lives with his fiancee. June is 30 and married, with five sons. Jennifer is 29 and unmarried. Jonathon was the next born and would now have been 27. However he was killed in a car accident four years previously. Michelle, the youngest in the family is aged 20, and lives in a shared flat with friends. Joan and June do not work in paid employment outside the home, but Joan looks after two of her grandchildren while their parents are at work. Philip is currently unemployed and is said to have a long history of depression. Edward, Amanda and Jennifer all have highly paid professional occupations.

Donald has been spending two full days each week with Beryl at their home and spends the rest of the time in the nursing home. Joan, the eldest daughter, has been coordinating a rota of visits and care, which involves all of the family. This involves transporting Donald home twice a week, helping with his care when at home, taking Beryl to visit him twice a day at the nursing home and assisting Beryl with her own care at home. Social services report that there have been numerous conflicts about the rota, and various members of the family have phoned social services to complain that they are not able to visit as often as Joan's rota requires, and asking social services to 'do something' about this. Social services had initially suggested that the family members should discuss this with Joan, but this has led to disagreements in the family with no resolution. Various members of the family have also complained to staff and the manager of the nursing home, and to social services, about his care at the nursing home. They have variously complained that they feel staff at the home are 'not caring' enough, and that their father should receive more attention from staff. Staff at the home have advised social services that they have an individual care plan for Donald and they try to attend frequently to his care needs. They feel that the family have expectations of 24-hour one-to-one care, which is not necessary in their view, and they also find it difficult to attend to his needs during his family's frequent visits as they report that the family interfere with this, and that the family either try to provide this care themselves or tell the staff how to attend to their father throughout this time.

Genogram:
The genogram may appear as shown on the opposite page.

From the genogram it can be seen that Donald and Beryl had their first daughter, Joan, when Beryl was 20 and their last child, Michelle, when Beryl was 43. With the exception of June, none of their children has chosen to have a large number of children, as Donald and Beryl did. Beryl had her first four pregnancies in rapid succession, followed

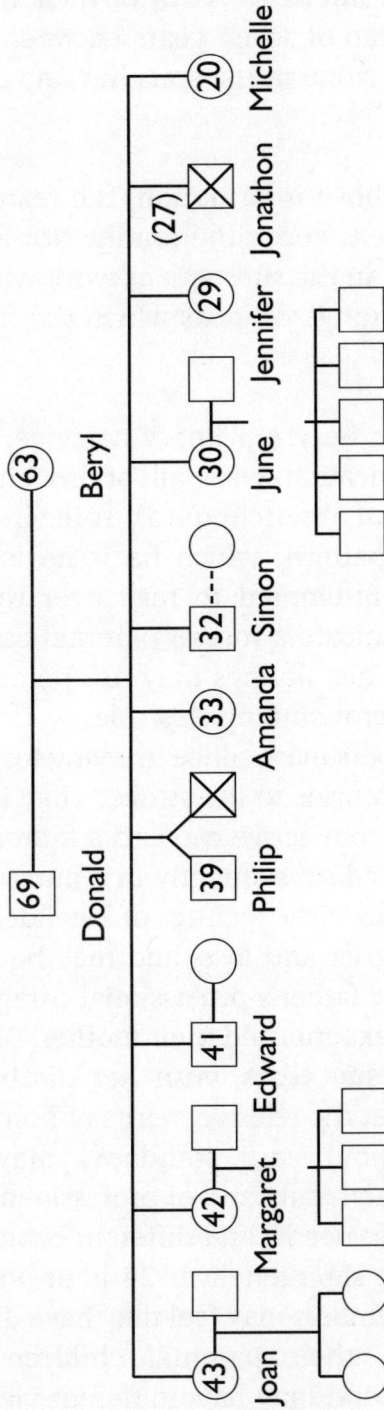

by a gap of six years after the death of their baby son (Philip's twin brother). There is a gap of seven years between the birth of Jonathon and that of Michelle. None of the sons has any children at present.

Hypotheses
On the basis of the above information, the team generated a number of hypotheses and ideas about the family. Not all of these ideas were discussed or explored in the subsequent work with this family, but they helped to generate a range of ideas which the therapists took into the sessions with them.

- Donald had been Beryl's primary caregiver and had also kept in regular communication with all of his children. He may have played a pivotal 'switchboard' role in this large family's communication pattern, which he is no longer able to achieve. Joan may have attempted to take over this role and has been trying to communicate a rota of parental care to her brothers and sisters. However her siblings may not perceive this as her role or be happy with her assuming this role.

- The family members may still be grieving for the loss of their father as they knew him prior to the stroke. They have experienced their father changing from active carer to a father with disabilities, in a hospital setting and subsequently in a nursing home. They may be experiencing some of the feelings of bewilderment and anger often associated with grief and loss, and may be directing some of this externally at their father's professional caregivers.

- The family have experienced their mother, Beryl, being cared for at her home for many years, with her disabilities, and may have strong views about the relative merits of home and residential care. Their beliefs about care standards may relate to different expectations of the family and of professional staff as to the type of care which Donald needs, and different conclusions about whether the nursing home should deliver 24-hour one-to-one care.

- Various family members may feel they have different responsibilities with respect to their parents, children, grandchildren and spouse/partners, and may have different views about the amount of time which caring for relatives and paid work should take up in their lives. This may be creating conflicts of time and divided loyalties concerning caregiving, and may be accompanied by a range of emotions, such as feelings of inadequacy, anger and guilt.

- Beryl and Donald are disabled at a relatively young age and their children may have fears about their own health and care in the future when they reach a similar age.
- There is a wide age range in Donald and Beryl's children, which may place them at different stages of the life cycle. Although they are all experiencing the same life cycle event with respect to caring for disabled and ageing parents, they may each be experiencing very different life cycle events too. Some of these events may be 'centripetal', and others may be 'centrifugal' (see Chapter 5).
- This is a large family with wide age gaps between the siblings. There may be a number of well established allegiances between siblings which may be important to understanding the current family system of care for their parents, and their respective willingness to accept Joan's rota for care.

The family team invited Donald, Beryl and all of their children to an initial family meeting. We also invited them to bring along anyone else they felt might wish to contribute to the session. The team considered inviting a representative from social services and/or from the nursing home. However some family members had met social services and nursing home staff in the past at a case conference about Donald's care. In order to try to make this session different from a formal case review, and also because of the logistics of a meeting with such a large group, it was decided to invite the family only for this appointment with the family team.

Beryl, Joan, Margaret, Edward, June, Jennifer and Michelle attended. Joan's eldest daughter, Alice, also attended, with her two young children. There were therefore 10 family members and two therapists present. It is often interesting to reflect upon reasons for absent members not attending, and the two therapists did talk briefly with the family about this during the session. What would your hypotheses be about the non-attendance of family members, and what are your ideas about Alice being the only grandchild to attend? Some of the issues which seemed important to this family are outlined below.

Donald: the family feeling they should 'protect' him; not wishing to say in front of him things which may upset him; not knowing how to communicate with him; not knowing how much he will understand.
Amanda: lives overseas.
Philip: has experienced mental health problems and depression himself; may be reluctant to attend for an appointment in a mental health services setting.
Simon: is engaged to be married and busy with wedding plans and work (centrifugal forces?); gender issues – sons not expected to offer as much care – or concerned that they may become the sole carer, as Donald did?
Alice: attended to support Joan, as Joan looks after Alice's children while Alice works, as well as playing a key role in caring for Beryl and Donald.

The session began with the family being asked what they hoped to achieve from the meeting with the family team. This was an open question, to which Joan responded first. She described how she had tried to organise a rota so that her father and mother felt they were well supported and cared for. She felt that some family members were contributing well (Margaret and June) but that others were 'not pulling their weight'. She felt that family members she perceived as having fewer other responsibilities played the smallest part in caring for their parents. She talked, supported by her daughter, Alice, about how she had had to do 'extra shifts on the rota' because other family members had 'let her down'. Margaret and June supported her position and directed anger at other family members. Joan felt her parents had had a difficult time raising a large family and now deserved their support in return. Jennifer and Michelle expressed appreciation of the support Joan was giving to their parents and expressed a willingness to continue helping, but they did not feel they could do as much as Joan's rota required them to do. This led to a prolonged verbal dispute between family members during the session, which the therapists allowed to evolve. After some time, Beryl interrupted. She asked them to each help as much as they could and reminded them that Donald had always insisted that they should 'lead their own lives' and that he had discouraged them from helping with Beryl's care in the past, when he had been her main carer prior to the stroke.

This led on to a productive discussion in which family members were able to discuss how much help they felt they could give. This required little intervention from the two therapists, other than to try to ensure that all family members' views were listened to. The therapists felt that this session provided an opportunity for members of this large family to meet and communicate about Donald and Beryl's care in a way which had not been possible previously. Donald had previously acted as the centre for communication in the family and could no longer do this. Joan had tried to take on this role but family members had not been comfortable with the rota which she employed as a coordinating communicatory device and Joan had found it impossible to communicate with all of the family to check their capacities with respect to caring for their parents as the logistics of this, in addition to her other responsibilities, were too much for her.

This family had had to deal with difficult events in the past, such as Jonathon's death and Beryl's disabilities, and had done so without seeking help from services. On this occasion the family session served the function of bringing the family together so that they could generate their own solutions. The therapists played an enabling role. This family were seen on a further occasion, when they continued to discuss how they could best care for Beryl and Donald and were encouraged by the therapists to reflect upon their expectations of the standard of care which the nursing home could provide, and how they might resolve this aspect. They were then offered a further appointment, but Joan subsequently contacted the family team to say that the family had asked her to cancel the appointment as they felt they had resolved things following the second session and had got together as a family themselves. They had evolved a series of visits, but not a rota, which family members could cope with and would contact us in the future if this broke down. To date they have not done so and Donald remains at the same nursing home.

In the course of running a family clinic for older adults and their families, the team with which I work has developed a range of administrative materials, questionnaires and information sheets. Examples of these sheets appear below. They are used to provide information about the service, to help in administering the clinic and to assist in auditing the practice of the clinic.

We have tried to work towards a unified approach, where the service offered by the family team complements that offered by other parts of the mental health services for older adults in our area. This involves a process of networking and cross-referral. Clients attending the clinic may gain access to other services as a result of attending the clinic, as members of our team have access to, for example, hospital inpatient beds, day hospital services and social services resources by way of the medical and social services workers with our team. Developing the team has also involved a process of finding out about other statutory and non-statutory services, so that we are aware of the range of services which can be offered to older adults and their families. Multidisciplinary working has always been an important part of the team's work and philosophy, and the family team has always included members from a wide range of disciplines and therapeutic backgrounds. We feel that this enriches the approaches we can offer to families, and the diverse backgrounds of team members also allows a healthy exchange of ideas in the team, which enables team members to develop their own knowledge and skills.

The team with which I work runs a number of workshops concerning the practice of family/systems therapy with older adults and their families, and also runs workshops which are designed to help individuals or teams who are considering offering a family therapy service themselves. One of the issues which others often raise in these circumstances is that of resources, and how they may justify the costs of working with families to managers, referrers and others, particularly if the service is offered by a team of people. One of the dilemmas here is that a family approach may be particularly appropriate and most cost effective when working with families who are 'stuck' and who are utilising a wide range of expensive resources. In such cases difficulties may not have been resolved by adopting an individual client approach.

However 'beginning teams' may find this kind of work initially overwhelming and may find it more developmentally helpful to work with more 'straightforward' families. This may initially be perceived as an expensive way of offering a service.

When our team began working together we tried to work with 'straightforward' families, if there can be such a thing, where changes at least seemed to be more readily achievable. We tried not to work very often with families where the situation appeared to have been 'stuck' for some time. We often worked with families where the older person was already known to our service and where family work was an adjunct to other work with the client. This enabled our co-worker therapists to develop skills in working together and allowed a gradual development of the service from one which offered occasional family work to one which became more formal and offered specific family clinic sessions to which other clinicians could refer clients. This also allowed and enabled a gradual assimilation of ideas about family working into the system with which we work. As the work began to be perceived as helpful to this system, it enabled us to develop the service without major reservations being expressed by others about its value in terms of cost effectiveness.

This may be a privileged position in which to work, particularly in the healthcare market-place which operates today. It is, however, an example of the way services which can gradually establish their likely benefits, which begin to attract interest from potential referrers and which incorporate contributions from a range of different staff disciplines may often become an accepted part of a service and be supported in developing further.

CHAPTER 9

Administrative Material

Information Sheet: 'About Our Service'
This provides a brief outline of the family service, its address, location, telephone number and brief details about what the service does and how we work. It is sent in booklet form to all family members who are invited to attend for an appointment, and is also available as an information sheet for family doctors, social services and other potential referrers to the service.

Information Sheet

MAP   TITLE OF
                                        THE SERVICE

ADDRESS _____

        _____

        _____

How Can We Help?
We provide a service for families with older adult members. The team is made up of a number of mental health care professionals.

Experience shows that as families age and change, difficulties may arise needing extra help or support. Problems that may need help include:

- bereavement
- marital difficulties
- retirement
- adjusting to illness
- moving home
- stresses and strains of caring, and many more.

These difficulties can affect all members of the family and this is why we like to meet all those involved when possible.

How Do We Contact Families?
Families may be referred by their doctors, social workers, community nurses and other professionals involved with them. Families can approach the service themselves for further information about referral.

We normally write to invite each family member to a meeting at a resource centre. You are welcome to bring along people important to you or your family, who are not family members.

If there are problems with transport, or getting to the clinic we may be able to help. Our family service administrator (Name: Tel:) can advise about this and other questions you may have.

How Do We Work?
Usually two members of the team work with the family for about an hour. With support from our colleagues we can often help a family to take a fresh look at both the family's situation and each person's position within it. This can often lead on to significant change.

Family Registration Form

This is a sheet with basic demographic details of the older adult member of the family. The service has varied its practice over the years and no longer asks each family member to complete registration details. A single family case file is now produced on the basis of the family registration form shown below and this is completed using details from the referred older adult family member only:

SURNAME _____ SURNAME AT BIRTH _____

FIRST NAME _____ DATE OF BIRTH _____

ADDRESS _____

_____

_____

TEL. NO. _____

I AM (*PLEASE TICK*):

SINGLE ☐   MARRIED ☐   WIDOWED ☐

LIVING WITH A PARTNER ☐   DIVORCED ☐   SEPARATED ☐

MY NEXT OF KIN IS:

NAME _____ RELATIONSHIP _____

ADDRESS _____

_____

MY FAMILY DOCTOR IS:

DR _____

ADDRESS _____

_____

THANK YOU FOR COMPLETING THIS FORM.

Attendance Record Sheet

This sheet is stapled into the inside of the family casenotes and provides an 'at a glance' record of when the family were offered appointments in the clinic and whether they attended. The sheet also documents whether a letter was sent to the referrer, how often the family were seen by the service and when the family were discharged from the service. This record sheet helps in administering the clinic, and is also useful for audit purposes.

NAME _____ CASE NOTES NUMBER _____

SESSION NUMBER	DATE	OUTCOME attended cancelled DNA	LETTER SENT TO REFERRER	APPT MADE?	DISCHARGED ?

Videotape Agreement Form

This is a formal consent form relating to the use of video recordings of family clinic therapeutic sessions. The use of video recordings is discussed with families who attend the clinic. In the course of introducing the family to the clinic set-up at the beginning of the first appointment, the therapists also ask for the families' permission to switch on the video recorder at the beginning of the appointment. They explain that the use of video recording obviates the need for detailed note taking and that it provides a confidential record of the session, which may be usefully employed to review change later. The therapists explain that, if the family are happy for the video to be switched on, they will be asked at the end of the session whether they are happy for the video recording of the session to be retained. This final formal consent, using the video agreement form, is sought at the end of the session, as the family will then know what the content of the session has been. They are then in a better position to decide whether they are happy for the recording of the session to be retained. If any family member decides not to sign the consent form, then the video tape of the session is deleted. In practice very few families decline to give video consent.

Videotape Agreement Form

I/We agree to videotape recordings being made of our sessions at the family clinic.

I/We understand that these tapes may be used (please delete as appropriate):
(a) by our therapists and team to review the sessions in order to help us
(b) by our therapists and team as part of the family clinic training of other professional people. Excerpts from videos will only be used at the discretion of your therapists and only in the presence of professional people

I/We agree that these tapes may be used

(a) without limit of time _____

(b) until _____

SIGNATURES OF FAMILY MEMBERS _____

_____

_____

_____

_____

Videotapes are held securely and we take every precaution to safeguard your confidentiality.

THERAPIST _____

DATE _____

Peer Consultant Sheet

This is a sheet completed by the peer consultant of the session. The role of the peer consultant was described in Chapter 1. The name of the family, date of attendance, number of session, names of therapists and consulting team are recorded. A seating plan of where family members sat in the session is drawn. Brief notes are made about the discussion during the 'time out' period when the therapists leave the family to consult colleagues, before returning to meet the family again (see page 10). The plan for future contact with the family is also briefly noted. The peer consultant has the responsibility for producing a letter for the referrer and uses these details as the basis for the letter.

Family Clinic Peer Consultant Sheet

FAMILY _____

DATE _____

SESSION _____

THERAPISTS _____

PEER CONSULTANT _____

CONSULTING TEAM _____

SEATING PLAN

CONTENT OF TIME OUT DISCUSSION _____

_____

_____

PLAN _____

_____

_____

Letter to the Referrer

At the end of each appointment, a letter is sent by the peer consultant, on behalf of the family team, to the referrer, and to the family doctor (if the doctor is not the referrer). Standard headings are used for this.

Dear Dr/Ms/Mr _____

RE: _____

The above person attended the family clinic on: _____

Family members present: _____

Family members invited but did not attend: _____

Therapists: _____

_____

Reason for meeting: _____

_____

_____

Summary of meeting: _____

_____

_____

_____

Team formulation of the family: _____

_____

_____

Plan: _____

_____

_____

Yours Sincerely, _____

On behalf of the family team.

Therapist Questionnaire

This questionnaire has been used by the family team for audit purposes and also in research analyses concerning the family clinic. It records basic demographic information, information about the referred older adult and about those who attended the clinic. The questionnaire also records the range of therapeutic techniques which were used in each session, and a range of topics which were discussed during the session. This allows consideration of the way working practices in the clinic may change over time, and also how the topics discussed and presented by families may change over time. From a review of these aspects of the questionnaire, our service has been able to determine, for example, that we are much more likely to use systemic techniques, such as positive reframes and circular questions, than when we first began the clinic, and are much less likely to use structural techniques, such as structural moves. The topics discussed and presented in family sessions have also changed and the total number of areas of difficulty which are discussed has increased over time. Discussion of topics such as family rifts, suicide, alcohol and drugs problems and elder abuse have all increased, whereas topics such as retirement, bereavement and forgetfulness have changed very little. This sort of information allows a process audit of the nature of the work within the clinic and can be a very helpful way of reflecting upon changing working practices and priorities in the clinic. Notes to aid the completion of the questionnaire are presented at the end, and describe what the team understand the various therapeutic techniques to be.

The therapist questionnaire also records what the follow up arrangements for the family were, and makes a simple attempt to rate subjectively the outcome of the session from the perspective of the team. A therapist questionnaire is completed at the end of each family clinic appointment with a family, and takes about five minutes to complete. The use of the therapist questionnaire is described in Benbow *et al* (1993).

Therapist Questionnaire

PATIENT SURNAME _____

PATIENT FORENAME _____

GENDER OF REFERRED PERSON

1   Male   2   Female

DATE OF BIRTH _____

DATE OF THIS SESSION _____

NUMBER OF THIS SESSION _____

NUMBER OF THERAPISTS _____

GENDER AND NAME OF THERAPISTS

1   Male _____

2   Female _____

WHERE SEEN FOR THIS SESSION

1   Clinic Base   ☐   4   Nursing/Residential Home   ☐

2   Own Home   ☐   5   Ward   ☐

3   Relative's Home   ☐   6   Other _____

FAMILY MEMBERS SEEN IN THIS SESSION AND NAMES

1   Referred Person   _____

2   Spouse/Partner   _____

3   Son   _____

4   Daughter   _____

5   Son-in-law   _____

6   Daughter-in-law   _____

7   Brother   _____

8   Sister   _____

9   Brother-in-law   _____

10   Sister-in-law   _____

11   Granddaughter   _____

12   Grandson   _____

13   Niece   _____

14   Nephew   _____

15   Other (relationship
     and name)   _____

WHICH OF THE FOLLOWING WERE USED WITH THE FAMILY?

(Circle all which apply).

1   Genogram

2   Circular questioning

3   Transgenerational Analysis

4   Exploring family myths

5   Therapist assigned to ally
    with family member(s)

6   Drama work

7   Role play

8   Role reversal

9   Sculpting

10   Empty chair

11   Positive reframe

12   Prescribing symptom

13   Paradox

14   Split message

15   Structural moves

16   Task setting

    (a) intra-session

    (b) extra-session

17   Modelling

18   Other (please specify)

     _____

WHICH OF THE FOLLOWING WERE DISCUSSED DURING THE SESSION? (Circle all that apply.)

1   Referred person's physical health

2   Other family member's physical health

3   Other family member's mental health

4   Referred person's behavioural problems

5   Referred person's forgetfulness/confusion

6   Bereavement

7   Decision about change of residence

8   Long-standing family rift

9   'Leaving home' issue

10 Marital problems (referred person and spouse)

11 Marital problems (other family members)

12 Suicidal ideas/action

13 Seeking medical solutions (eg tablets)

14 Recent change in time spent together

15 Financial concerns (any family members)

16 Unemployment (of family members)

17 Alcohol problems

18 Drugs problems

19 Difficulty controlling anger/temper

20 Housing problem

21 Retirement

22 Referred person's sensory deficit

23 Problems associated with work/employment

24 Abuse or neglect of referred person

25 Sexuality

26 Death

27 Expressing emotion

28 Domestic violence/abuse of other person

29 Redundancy

30 Loneliness

31 Leaving hospital

32 Social activities

33 Religion

34 Cross culturalisation/ethnicity

35 Adoption

36 Other _____

WERE ANY OF THE FOLLOWING EVIDENT DURING THE SESSION?

1 Family 'enmeshed'

2 Family 'disengaged'

3 Reluctance of family to involve referred person

4 Family secret(s)

5 Therapist part of the system

6 Recurring patterns across generations

7 Social status differences in the family

8 Selective deafness/selective use of sensory impairment

WAS VIDEO USED?   YES   NO   DON'T KNOW

FOLLOW UP AFTER SESSION

0   None

1   Family clinic

2   Follow-up by team member (specify)

3   Routine psychiatric follow-up only

4   Routine psychiatric follow-up and team member follow up (specify)

5   Other service offered (eg, day hospital) but only if as a result of family

clinic decision (specify)

6   Discharge

SUBJECTIVE ATTITUDE OF TEAM TO THE SESSION

Referred person assisted	Not at all	A little	Moderately	Considerably
Family assisted	Not at all	A little	Moderately	Considerably
Team assisted	Not at all	A little	Moderately	Considerably

Were any outside agencies assisted?   YES   NO   DON'T KNOW

Please state which agencies were assisted _____

Notes to Aid Completion of the Therapist Questionnaire

1 **Genogram:** pictorial family tree.
2 **Circular questioning:** questions designed to elicit information to understand better the connectedness of the system, for example asking a family member what another family member would have said/done.
3 **Transgenerational analysis:** looking at patterns/links recurring across generations.
4 **Family myths:** a body of beliefs that the family has about itself and its members which has some stability conferred by having been repeatedly confirmed by family consensus over the years: for example, 'All people who move to hospital die' or 'Expressing sadness will lead to madness/loss of control' and so on.
5 **Therapist assigned to ally with family member:** the team have agreed to this as part of the therapeutic plan.
6 **Drama work:** enacting or re-enacting situations by way of drama work/part playing within the family session.
7 **Role-play:** a family member is asked to role play within the family session, or the therapist uses role-play to demonstrate something in the session.
8 **Role reversal:** therapist and client or two family members reverse roles and actively play the new role in the session.
9 **Sculpting:** asking family members to adopt particular positions/postures.
10 **Empty chair:** a chair is left intentionally vacant for an absent member.
11 **Positive reframe:** relabelling an action, statement or thought, positively: for example, 'Your anger shows your concern' , 'Your action is protecting your mother.'
12 **Prescribing symptoms:** prescribing/telling the person to continue with their symptom: for example, 'We think you will continue to be ill/not take your tablets', and so on.
13 **Paradox:** an intervention which, if followed, will accomplish the opposite of what it is seemingly intended to accomplish. Giving a

message which it is intended the family member(s) will resist/do the opposite of/act in a different way from.

14 **Split message:** the team present a message but one member/some members of the team present an alternative message or viewpoint to the family.

15 **Structural moves:** these include asking the family members and/or therapists to change chairs; asking family members to speak directly to one another rather than to the therapist; delineating boundaries.

16 **Task setting:** (a) intra-session: for example, give family a task to do during the session;
(b) extra-session: for example, give the family a task to do before the next session.

17 **Modelling:** the therapist models/demonstrates a different emotional or behavioural response to a given situation.

18 **Other(s):** be over- rather than under-inclusive.

References

Anderson T, 1990, *The Reflecting Team. Dialogues and Dialogues about the Dialogues,* Borgman, Broadstairs Kent.

Barker P, 1983, *Basic Family Therapy,* Granada, London.

Barnhill LM & Longo D, 1978, 'Fixation and Regression in the Family Life Cycle', *Family Process* 17, pp 469-478.

Benbow SM, Marriott A, Morley M & Walsh S, 1993, 'Family Therapy and Dementia: Review and Clinical Experience', *International Journal of Geriatric Psychiatry* 8, pp 717-725.

Blenkner M, 1965, 'Social Work and Family Relationships in Later Life with some Thoughts on Filial Maturity', Shanas E & Streib G (eds), *Social Structure and the Family,* Prentice Hall, Englewood Cliffs, New Jersey.

Bloch DA, 1993, 'Foreword', in Jones E, *Family Systems Therapy. Developments in the Milan-Systemic Therapies,* Wiley, Chichester.

Bowen M, 1978, *Family Therapy in Clinical Practice,* Ronson, New York.

Burnham J, 1986, *Family Therapy: First Steps Towards a Systemic Approach,* Tavistock Library of Social Work Practice, Routledge, London.

Carpenter J, 1993, 'Working Together', Carpenter J & Treacher A (eds), *Using Family Therapy in the 90's,* Basil Blackwell Oxford.

Carpenter J & Treacher A (eds), 1993, *Using Family Therapy in the 90's,* Basil Blackwell, Oxford.

Carter B & McGoldrick M (eds), 1989, *The Changing Family Life Cycle: A Framework for Family Therapy,* (2nd edn), Allyn & Bacon, Boston.

Cecchin G, 1987, 'Hypothesising, Circularity and Neutrality Revisited. An Invitation to Curiosity', *Family Process* 26, 4, pp 405-413.

Combrinck-Graham L, 1985, 'A Developmental Model For Family Systems', *Family Process* 24, pp 139-150.

Dunham PJ, 1977, *Experimental Psychology: Theory and Practice*, Harper and Row, London.

Duvall EM, 1977, *Marriage and Family Development* (5th edn), J.B. Lippincott, Philadelphia.

Griffin WA, 1993, *Family Therapy: Fundamentals of Theory and Practice*, Brunner/Mazel, New York.

Hoffman L, 1990, 'Introductory Foreword', Anderson T, *The Reflecting Team. Dialogues and Dialogues about the Dialogues*, Borgman, Broadstairs Kent.

Hughes S, Berger M & Wright L, 1978, 'The Family Life Cycle and Clinical Intervention', *Journal of Marriage and Family Counselling* 5, pp 33-40.

Lieberman S, 1979, *Transgenerational Family Therapy*, Croom Helm, London.

O'Brien J, 1981, *The Principle of Normalisation. A Foundation for Effective Services*, CMHERA, London.

Palazzoli-Selvini M, Boscolo L, Cecchin G & Prata G, 1980, 'Hypothesising, Circularity, Neutrality: Three Guidelines for the Conductor of the Session', *Family Process* 19, 1, pp 3-12.

Penn P, 1982, 'Circular Questioning', *Family Process* 21, 3, pp 267-280.

Perlman D, 1988, 'Loneliness: A Life Span, Family Perspective', Milardo RM (ed), *Families and Social Networks*, Sage, London.

Ratna L & Davis J, 1984, 'Family Therapy with the Elderly Mentally Ill. Some Strategies and Techniques', *British Journal of Psychiatry* 145, pp311-315.

Smith D & Kingston P, 1980, 'Live Supervision without a One Way Screen', *Journal of Family Therapy* 2, pp 379-387.

Street E & Dryden W (eds), 1988, *Family Therapy in Britain*, OU Press, Milton Keynes.

Tomm K, 1988, 'Interventive Interviewing Part 3: Intending to ask Linear, Circular, Strategic or Reflective Questions?', *Family Process* 27, pp 1-15.

Walsh F, 1989, 'The Family In Later Life', Carter B & McGoldrick M (eds), *The Changing Family Life Cycle: A Framework for Family Therapy* (2nd edn), Allyn & Bacon, Boston.

Wenger GC, 1984, *The Supportive Network: Coping with Old Age*, Allen & Unwin, London, 1984.